Praise for Linda Leigh Francis

"A GREAT READ! Linda is an astute business person whose method of teaching is laced with humor and insight. Her book is the best I've read on common sense solutions for your business. It's loaded with wise and practical methods of making your way in this fast paced, sometimes befuddling business world."

— Sue Salinas, Executive Director,
Sonoma County Executive Association

"Over the course of two years, Linda Francis coached me on the principles outlined in her book. I have wished since then that I had a handy resource that I could refer to when the going gets tough. Thanks to you, Linda, for putting it all in writing in one place."

— Dave Carter, Owner, Great Harvest Bakery

"Linda has taught the class that is the basis of this book at the Builders Exchange since 1991. In this time she has educated over 100 construction companies — on how to run their companies successfully and profitably. It's all here in her book."

— Larry Dashiell, Owner, Summit Electric
and President of North Coast Builders Exchange

"I am delighted that Linda has put her course into book form. The 'Time Management' segment was worth the whole course for me. It helped me establish priorities and organize my life *and* business in a way that increased my earnings considerably. I continue to refer to my notes and to use them as a refresher course on an annual basis."

— April Tweddell, GRI, Co-Owner, Pacific Properties.

"Linda's book is a straightforward and sensible business approach that gives you the strategies you need to run your business, simply and effectively. We know. We did it!!! Steve and Sue AKA Art and Mary Crane."

— Art and Mary Crane, Crane and Son Plumbing and Heating

"Running a retail business requires making tough decisions every day. This book is like having a business consultant at your fingertips. It is a constant resource on my shelf. It's so reassuring to have simple direct answers to the everyday questions. It is must reading for every manager who wants to improve their business while improving their lives."

— Nancy Hensley, Manager Real Goods Retail Store
at the Solar Living Center, Hopland CA.
"The Country Store of the Future."

"This book is an excellent practical guide for starting or growing a business. I strongly recommend it as a 'must read' for those who are in business or about to start a new venture. It offers a step by step plan for being organized and being successful. Many of us are searching for ways to improve our businesses and the economic health of our communities. I recommend this book as a good place to begin the search."

— Patti Campbell, Fourth District Supervisor, Mendocino County

"One of the biggest advantages to Linda's seminars was identifying and systematizing what is incredibly obvious, but is always overlooked. Specifically, I am referring to the job descriptions being intricately tied to the performance review. That service was worth enough to pay for the entire consulting contract I had with Linda. You will find specific details on how to make this program work inside."

— Richard P. Selzer, Realty World-Selzer Realty

RUN YOUR BUSINESS
SO IT DOESN'T RUN YOU

LINDA LEIGH FRANCIS

Borah Press
Redwood Valley, California

Borah Press

Phone (800) 222-0666 • fax (707) 485-7071 • e-mail: lfrancis@pacific.net

Cover design by Theresa Whitehill, Colored Horse Studios, Elk, CA
Nautilus logo by Dorothy O'Neill
Page design and book production by Cypress House, Fort Bragg, CA 95437

Some material has been reproduced from *50 Activities for Developing Leaders,* written by Lois B. Hart, Ed.D., copyright 1994. Reprinted by permission of the publisher, HRD Press, Inc., 22 Amherst Rd., Amherst, MA 01002, 1-800-822-2801, (413) 253-3488, fax 413-253-3490.

Publisher's Cataloging-in-Publication
(Provided by Quality Books, Inc.)
Francis, Linda Leigh.
Run your business so it doesn't run you / Linda
Leigh Francis. --Rev. ed.
p.   cm.
Includes bibliographical references.
LCCN: 99-97636
ISBN: 0-9657879-1-5
1. Small business--Management.   2. Time management.
I. Title.
HD62.7.F73 2000   658.02'2
                                       QBI00-268

Manufactured in the USA
3 5 7 9 8 6 4 2

RUN YOUR BUSINESS

SO IT DOESN'T RUN YOU

DEDICATION

This book is dedicated to all the great people in my workshops and consulting relationships who have shared their businesses and their lives with me. And who took the leap — into more successfully businesses and balanced lives.

CONTENTS

Chapter 5: Cash Is King

Chapter 6: Planning Your Future

Chapter 7: Opening Your Books
With Open Book Management

Chapter 8: Who Do You Need?

Chapter 9: Finding the Right People

Chapter 10: Keeping The Best Of The Bunch

Chapter 11: Keeping Your Company Legal

Chapter 12: Now You Have to Sell It

Chapter 13: Taking The Leap

Introduction

To a weary horse, even his tail is a burden.

— Czech proverb

Sue and Steve Baker have taken care of the heating, cooling and plumbing problems in their small town for over 15 years. Their yellow page ad informs customers they've been "In Business for over 50 Years", because Steve's dad founded Baker and Sons that many years ago. When the old man retired, Steve and his wife took over the helm.

At first, the company provided the Bakers and their six employees with a decent living, but running the busy service company soon became all work and no play. Sue and Steve began wondering if they were really getting ahead or just treading water. Running the office consumed all of Sue's time, and because Steve was so busy doing service calls, he barely had the time to do estimates. They couldn't even think about changing-over to the latest technology or doing ongoing employee training. To make matters worse, some of Sue and Steve's employees made as much money as they, and the employees didn't take any work home with them at night!

Then one dreadful day, a long term employee called in and quit, just like that. To make matters worse, he was their nephew. "Your business is so disorganized," he said. "Why, I can do it better myself." And in fact, he was going out to do just that.

Sue and Steve were stunned. "He never even complained," Sue said. "He never told us anything was wrong."

Steve chimed in, "He's my nephew, where's his sense of loyalty? Besides, he's a plumber. He doesn't know how to run a service business. He'll ruin us both!"

"He's right about morale though," Sue remarked. "Everyone is so down. I thought owning a business was going to be fun. What went wrong? Why are we working so hard and getting nowhere? We deserve better than this."

Steve and Sue are not alone. Thousands of business owners and managers work long hours, earn meager profits or sustain mounting losses, endure unreliable employees, and suffer burnout and fatigue. They are great at their skill or trade and produce great products and services, but they finally give it up, because it all becomes just too much.

Fortunately, Sue and Steve decided to do something about their problems. They knew they had to do things differently, and they were determined to succeed. They decided it was time to *run their business so it didn't run them.*

In my seminars and consulting relationships I have met hundreds of people like Sue and Steve. They've told me that they wished they'd had the information contained in this book years ago. I wrote this book for them. I want to reach them before they spend any more sleepless nights worrying about whether their employees have security or their enterprise has any kind of future at all.

Even though writing this book took a lot of time, energy, and dedication, there was no stopping it. I kept seeing the looks of anguish on the faces of Sue and Steve when they registered for one of my seminars. I knew that with a little direction from me, and a great deal of diligence on their part, they could turn their business around and enjoy life. So can you.

I've had the privilege of working with plumbing contractors and tile contractors, manufacturers and engineers, energy experts and electricians, Realtors, roofers, retailers, insurance agents, auto repair people, accountants and employment counselors, and builders and bakers. I have seen highly skilled people working in chosen professions enjoying the fruits of their labor.

I have also met fine people working *too* hard, who are not smiling enough nor having enough to show for their years of labor. I have met people who felt used, abused, and unappreciated by their employees, people without enough time to enjoy their families, friends, spouses, and hobbies, and people stressed-out and burned-out.

By identifying problems and applying solutions learned from my workshops and consulting relationships, people like Sue and Steve experience "aha's!", the light going on, the smiles returning, and the energy and fun coming back to them and their business. They enjoy increased profitability, form partnerships with their employees, and see control returning to their lives and business. Most important, there is once again joy, fun, and camaraderie.

What made the difference? They are great at their skill, producing their product, and supplying their service. What had been missing was how to manage the business of their business. They learned how to manage their time and their people, understand their financial information, and make a plan for where they wanted to be. Instead of constantly reacting, they learned how to create their future by being proactive in their actions. They began to make choices that worked for them. *Instead of reacting to what they got, they began going after what they wanted.*

These people chose to take the time to learn how to manage their business, and then they *applied* what they had learned.

Learning how to manage your business will take time, energy, diligence, and discomfort. The results will pay you back for your efforts many times over. There will be times you don't think you can make the changes. But, what do you really have to lose? The headaches, the heartaches, and the heartburn?

What do Sue and Steve have now? In four years their business has almost doubled in size. More important, it has increased its profitability. What they take home, their personal draw, has doubled. They now have ten employees. Sue manages the business more easily, and Steve now has the time to do estimates and to train employees. Their employees have learned what makes the business profitable and are all pulling in that direction.

However, the biggest difference is that Sue and Steve are in control and having a ball.

I designed this book to be a tool for managing your business, because I want your business to meet your needs. More detailed and extensive books on business management are available, but my goal is to give you information in such a way that you can use it immediately to get control of your business and your life. Once you implement what is in this book, you might even have the time to read some books. I've listed some great ones in the bibliography.

I know you are busy, so I kept this book short and to the point on purpose. I also designed it as a ready resource that you can go back to again and again to help you solve your challenges and problems. Read the book through once, and then chose which chapter needs to be your starting place. The key, of course, is to get started!

So now read on. Put a notebook by your side for jotting down ideas, your own "to do" lists, and the "assignments" at the end of each chapter.

It's time to take the leap.

Chapter 1

YOU AND YOUR BUSINESS

I still find each day too short for all the thoughts I want to think, all the walks I want to take, all the books I want to read and all the friends I want to see.

— John Burroughs

Small Businesses Are Growing

John Jones worked for a major US corporation for 26 years. He retired with a reasonable pension, a gold watch, and a real nice wall plaque. His son, John Jr. had always intended to follow in his Dad's footsteps, but John Jr. found it to be a whole new world out there.

It used to be that you got a job with a "parent" corporation and stayed with that company your whole working life. You worked for them. They took care of you. This was before the merger and acquisition frenzy of the eighties and the downsizing (or "rightsizing") of the nineties.

James E. Challenger, an outplacement specialist from Chicago, found that one of big business' major problems was a shortage of employees with good work ethic and company loyalty. Challenger commented, "It may be unrealistic to expect workers to possess these qualities since the employer cannot promise the same in return." Since big business offers little job security, more and more people are starting their own business. Included in this phenomenon are the women who start their own business because they are tired of hitting the glass ceiling, and because they want more time with their families. Of the millions of companies in the US, most have less than 20 employees, and one third of all businesses are owned by women. No wonder the small business arena is the fastest growing segment of the US economy.

People start their own business because they want the freedom to be their own boss, call their own shots, make their own mistakes, and control their own destiny. People love their professions and are convinced they can run a business just as well as anyone else. Or maybe it is just part of the American psyche to take advantage of our land of opportunity. So people take the leap.

Do You Know the Difference Between an Owner And a Worker?

Taking the leap from working in a business to managing and leading one is a much longer leap than most people imagine. They rent an office, hang out their shingle, hire an employee or two, and they are off and running. And running. And running. And running. Until one day they wake up exhausted, working for wages, and questioning their decision to start this #@*&!! business in the first place. Of the hundreds of thousands of small businesses that will start each year, close to half will not survive their first six years. Mostly, it is because the new owners don't know how to run a business.

Education and training rarely accompany the decision to move from employee to owner. Yet the skills needed for running a business are very much different from those needed to produce a product or service. Indeed, some skills that are useful at one level can be lethal at the other.

Let me give you some examples of what I mean. When you are an employee, it is advantageous to be one of the gang. As an owner or manager, you often need a more objective, bottom line approach. Some distance is needed. This is not to say that you are not supportive of your staff, but as your role changes, so does the nature of your relationships. You are no longer everyone's pal. You are the boss. You can be friendly, but not friends — a tough leap to make.

As a producer, attention to every detail is a strength. A short-term, get this job done focus is needed. To have this same perspective as an owner or manager can be deadly. You need to see the big picture from multiple perspectives and delegate the details. Trying to keep it all, do it all, see it all, know it all, can kill the business — and possibly the boss.

You must lay aside the technical expertise that was of such great value when you were an employee. In its place you will practice working through, and with employees, training *them* to be the experts, the producers. You no longer get to bake the cake. Now it is your job to see that it gets baked by well-trained bakers. Your job satisfaction will come from what others produce and their successes. Your success will be less immediate. This can be very frustrating. You may want to drop into your old employee role. You can't. It's not your job anymore.

As an employee, you expect to have all the information you need to do a good job. The job is clearly defined and has a beginning and an end. When done, you can stand back and see what you have accomplished. In contrast, an owner or manager needs to be able to do a good job with less than adequate information. At this level you need the ability to make quality decisions without sufficient information. Rarely are jobs clearly defined. You can effectively manage and lead all day long and not be able to stand back and see that you have done anything! Very frustrating!

Finally, as an employee, there is an end to your day. You hang up the tools and go home with the satisfaction of a job well-done. The owner gets to carry many of the worries home. Since much of what the owner does is think, you might not see the product of your daily effort for quite some time. Again, when you are on a new learning curve, the desire to go back to where you know what you are doing and can see what you have done is strong. Resist it!

Your Job Description As an Owner

What are some of the things you should be thinking about and doing? Here's the list. Get out your notebook and answer the following questions. This assessment will tell you how well you are doing each of these things now. When you have applied what is in this book, review these notes, and you will see how much better you are doing!

1. **Establishing your company's mission and direction.** Does your company have a clear mission? Is it in writing? Do your employees and customers know what it is?

2. **Creating your annual strategic plan.** Do you have an annual plan? Are you clear about where you are headed, and how you will get there? Are responsibilities for accomplishing the plan shared throughout the company?

3. **Effectively communicating the company mission and plan to all employees.** Are you letting your people know where you are going and how they can contribute? How and how often? Do your employees know how well the company is doing, and do they share in the effort and the success?

4. **Developing and monitoring your annual budget.** Are you working from a budget? Is it reflected on your profit and loss statement in a variance report? Do you use it to evaluate how well you are doing?

5. **Reviewing your financial information on a regular basis.** Are you looking at your balance sheet and profit and loss statement monthly? Do you know all they have to tell you? What about aging reports and cash flow projections? How do you use these tools to monitor the health of your business and your cash flow?

6. **Approving and making your capital expenditures.** What do you need, and when can you afford to buy it? Your cash flow budget and plan help you make these decisions.

7. **Determining personnel needs to accomplish your plan.** Who do you have, and who do you need? Are people in positions that maximize their contribution and justify what you are paying them? What are *you* doing, and is it the best use of your precious time?

8. **Making sure personnel is available to accomplish your plan.** Can you find the people you need when you need them? Do you find the really great employee? Do you hire and interview well?

9. **Creating personnel policies and benefit plans.** Have you thought through your personnel policies and practices to be sure they are attractive to employees, affordable for the company, and legal as well? Do your employees know what their benefits are?

10. **Assuring the adequacy of resources to achieve your plan.** Do you have what you need, when you need it? Do your people have the tools and materials to do the best job they can?

11. **Determining and implementing your marketing plan.** Do you know who you are, and how you are different from your competition? What is your competitive position?

12. **Assuring there is adequate work to meet company needs.** Are you spending the time to find the work, find the products, and make the sale? Or are sales and marketing something you avoid?

13. **Staying abreast of industry trends and issues.** Where is your industry headed? Are you on the cutting edge or bringing up the rear?

14. **Participating in industry associations.** Are you visible in your industry? What are you contributing?

15. **Promoting the company to the community.** Much of your business is based on relationships, referrals, and reputation. Do people know about you and about your business?

16. **Providing motivation and leadership to your employees.** How are you motivating your people? Is it working? Do you have a good team?

All of these things support the purpose of your job, which is to ensure that the company is prosperous and successful forever. If you are not performing the tasks on the owner's job description, you are not alone. You probably do not have the time, the right people in place to give you the time, or perhaps have yet to develop the skills you need. If your business is to be successful, you must tackle them.

Before we get into the nitty-gritty details, let's talk about leadership, because leadership is the glue that holds a successful company together.

Your Leadership Role

There is a difference between leadership and management. Leadership is vision and planning. Management is carrying out the vision and the plan. Leadership is securing the resources of people and things. Management is the effective use of those resources. Leadership is inspiration and motivation. Management is follow-through.

In a small company you may need to be both leader and manager, but it is critical that you wear the leadership hat on a regular basis.

Peter Drucker defines leadership and management in these ways: "Management is climbing the ladder of success. Leadership is making sure the ladder is leaning against the right wall." "Management is doing things right. Leadership is doing the right things."

My favorite description of the difference between leadership and management is by Stephen Covey in his book *Seven Habits of Highly Successful People.* He describes a company going through a very dense jungle. The producers are the ones wielding the machetes, hacking their way through the jungle. The managers are the ones insuring that the machetes are sharp and the supplies are there. The leader is the one who climbs the tallest tree, looks around and declares, "Wrong Jungle!"

I am reminded of a company that went out of business. Forty people lost their jobs. They were efficiently manufacturing 5 1/4 inch floppy disks. But, no one ever climbed the tallest tree to see if they were in the right jungle. They weren't. At that time, the jungle they should have been in was the 3-1/2 inch diskette's jungle.

It is your job as the leader of your company to be sure you are in the right jungle. At times this means you may have to make radical changes in direction. You may not get the support for needed change from your managers and producers. After all, they were so good at making 5-1/4 inch floppy disks. The only problem was, no one wanted them anymore. Wrong jungle!

Leaders are not always popular. But, *you* see the big picture, and *you* need to steer the ship — regardless of how upset people may get. Once you gather all the available information and solicit people's input, you get to make the decision. Your employees may or may not see the wisdom of your decision.

Make Sure the Business Meets Your Needs

Throughout all you do, always remember, this is *your* business, and it is *your* liability on the line. You need to be very clear about what *you* need from your business. This will help you to make good leadership decisions. So take some time right now, and think about what it is *you* want.

One way to do this is to imagine you only have six months to live. How would you spend your time? Or, think about what you want on your tombstone. If mine says, "She did some good and had some fun," I will die a happy woman. There are very few people on their deathbed who wish they had spent more time with their business. Maybe that's why in her work with the dying, Elizabeth Kubler Ross has found that people in the last months of their lives take up long forgotten pleasures like writing, painting, gardening, and reading.

One of the reasons you chose to have your own business is the freedom it offers you. Structure your business with this goal in mind. Whether you want to be small or large, local or international, known in your local community or in the whole world, build your business to meet all your needs — professional, personal, and spiritual.

You can do it. Honest!

Learn how to run your business. Don't let it run you. If you let it run you, you don't own a business. *You own a job* and a darn expensive one. So start with yourself. You are not being selfish. You are being wise. Keep your needs and your dreams in mind as you apply what you learn in this book, as you push through your comfort zones, as you change "the way we've always done it." Start with yourself; the only place to begin any journey.

The next two chapters on time management will give you some skills to get you started on this journey.

Your "TO DO" List

1. Think about what you want out of life. Think in terms of your business, your personal life, your family, and your spirit. Write these things down in your notebook.

2. What do you want your tombstone to say? Write it down in your notebook as well.

3. Begin reading a book on leadership. There are several in the bibliography.

4. Rate yourself from one (low) to ten (high) on the leadership traits on the following chart.

Leadership Traits   Score

√ Positive self image   _____
√ Self respect   _____
√ Self discipline   _____
√ Integrity   _____
√ Consistency   _____
√ Responsibility/reliability   _____
√ Strong ethics   _____
√ Passion for life   _____
√ Highly motivated to act   _____
√ Positive attitude   _____
√ Radiant physical health   _____

Chapter 2

DO YOU HAVE THE TIME?

The nature of man is always the same. It is their habits that separate them.

— Confucius

What Is Time?

What is time? — A measurement, a precious possession, a daily allotment, a valuable asset. It is perishable — something you cannot save, store, borrow or loan. If you are lucky, you will get another 24 hours of it tomorrow morning.

Time is money. There is never enough of it. It goes too fast, and sometimes it moves too slowly. There are 1440 minutes in a day — no more, no less. If you are fortunate enough to live to be 80 years old, you will receive 29,220 days of it. Finally, and this is very important to remember when you think about time management, no one can take it away from you unless you willingly give it up.

When I look at time in this way, suddenly time seems to be in short supply. It makes me want to be sure that I use this limited, precious possession the best way I possibly can. It helps me to overcome my natural resistance to changing how I do things.

We all make choices about how to use our precious time. If you truly want to manage *your* time, one of the first things you need to do is to control how you spend it. This comes down to the choices you make — or don't.

13

- *Do you change the merchandise display instead of asking your sales-clerk to do it?*

- *Do you do the engineering drawing instead of teaching people how to use the new software that will let them do it?*

- *Do you cook an elaborate dinner for your family instead of ordering Chinese take-out?*

- *Do you make up the daily work schedule instead of getting that important proposal out?*

- *Do you run errands an employee could do instead of scheduling that overdue performance review?*

- *Do you always respond when someone asks you a question, even though they really should know the answer?*

- *Do you always save the day when someone is about to fail?*

- *Do you always make excuses instead of getting it done?*

What choices are you making without thinking?

We often don't stop and think about the choices we make. Like Pavlov's dogs, we get the stimulus and we respond unthinkingly. Because we are human and not dogs, between the stimulus and the response, we have the opportunity to make a choice, to ask ourselves if this is really what we want to do with our time and energy. However, and this is very important, if you don't know where you are going, how do you decide? To make the most effective choice, you have to have goals.

Setting Your Goals

Studies have shown that people who set goals for themselves are more successful and prosperous. People who write their goals down are the most successful of all. Why is this? Well, for one thing, writing down what you want and where you are going helps you to make good, life choices. It helps you to say "No" to choices that do not move you in the direction you wish to go, and to recognize and say "Yes" to those choices that will help you get where you want to be.

If you don't have goals, there is a strong likelihood you will be spending your time working on the goals of someone who does have them. Wouldn't you rather have it the other way around?

Effective time management starts with goal setting. How do you set goals? The chapter on "Planning Your Future" discusses goal setting for your business. But, before you can set goals for your business, you need to set goals for yourself. What is it *you* want to do or have? Figure this out and write it down in your notebook. This can be very scary. Committing your goals to writing makes them real. This may be the first of many comfort zones you will need to go through. Once written, keep your goals where you can review them easily.

I have goals for my business, my family and myself. Every year in late December or early January, I set some time aside and write down my goals. I write these in the back of my appointment book, so I can refer to them frequently during the year, update them, or check them off. They help keep me focused on where I want to go and why. They help me to make *choices* on where to spend my precious time. Set some time aside to write your goals down, or it probably won't get done.

For your goals to be effective they need to be specific, measurable, and realistic. For example, I will read ten business related books this year. I will lose 15 pounds in the next six months. I will increase my sales by 10% or $XX this year. If I put 100 books, or 100 pounds, or a 100% increase in sales, the goals would be unrealistic and impossible to achieve. So, when you write down your goals, be specific about what they are and when you will accomplish them.

Your Basic Time Management Principles

There are different ways to use time. However, a business owner must spend time *planning and setting goals.* You must spend time *communicating* with the people around you, letting them know where you are going and why. And, you must spend time *directing* the activities of others, making sure they are doing the things necessary to help you get to where you are going. It is an unforgiving reality; a successful business owner must schedule time for planning, goal setting, communicating, and directing.

Let's look at it another way. As you move up in an organization, the ratio of how you spend your time between doing, managing, and leading shifts. If you are a front-line worker on a job, 100% of your time is spent doing. As a first level supervisor, 75% of your time is spent doing. You spend the other 25% of your time managing. This might be supervising an employee, determining material needs for the next day, or working with the manager on scheduling. As a manager, 50% to 80% of your time could be managing. This includes supervision of employees, scheduling, dealing with vendors and suppliers, materials acquisition, communication between the office, and so on.

When you get to be an owner, at least 90% of your time is managing and leading.

Remember the owner's job description? Go back to page 7 and review it. The things on that list refer to management and leadership. Unfortunately, many owners are so busy "doing" they never get to the critical, crucial, vital tasks of ownership — A big mistake. It is totally understandable.

Most small business owners start in the field, the front line — wherever it is — construction, retail, service, or manufacturing. They know how to produce the product, or service, or build the house. They are comfortable there. They are competent doing. But this ownership stuff is new, different, and hard, and they are clearly moving out of their comfort zone. Manage people? Review financial information? Do planning? Go schmooze? I'd rather hang Sheetrock. Plus, after working all day doing this ownership stuff, you can't stand back and see what you've done. There is little closure, especially if you have not set any goals.

So what they do, you do, we do, is gravitate back to our comfort zones, back to the "doing." We end up with 70% doing and maybe 50% managing and leading and wonder why we are working so hard and long, why our businesses are not going where we want, why our profits are low, and why our employees are so unproductive. If this in anyway describes your situation, it is time to restructure your company roles. Learn to delegate, push through some comfort zones, and start working on your business (managing and leading) instead of in it (doing).

A great way to start doing things differently is to get a truly clear picture of how you are actually spending your time. This brings us to the dreaded 15 minute time analysis. It means just what its name implies — keeping track of your time by 15 minute increments. This is a tool people love to hate. You won't like it either, but do it anyway. What it shows you will amaze or horrify you. The form to use follows. Here's how you use it.

Make ten copies of the form, one for each workday for two weeks. Keep a form with you each day, and note the activity you are doing in the left-hand column *as* you do it. If you do something in the morning and then go back to the activity later in the day, do not write it down again. Go back to the original line and fill in the time there. This will help you to see if you are bouncing around.

For example, a construction subcontractor did his bidding activity in 15 to 30 minute intervals throughout the whole day. He not only spent more time doing the job by doing it in 15 minute bits, he also created multiple opportunities for costly errors. The analysis gave him a good idea where to start managing his time differently. Now he creates two-hour blocks of time twice a week to get this critical job done. (On the following pages review the example of a well-managed day versus one that is out of control.)

If you forget to fill the sheet out for several hours, as best you can, go back and recreate how you spent the time. However, track your time as much as possible while you are going through the day.

At the end of the day, add up all the 15 minute increments and put the total time in the right-hand column. At the end of the two weeks, total the time you spent in each category. I find it useful to turn these into percentages.

Now analyze how you spent your time. Were you doing more than managing? Did you spread projects over the whole day rather than sitting down and just getting them done? Are you spending too much time in the car? Did you spend enough time marketing? Does how you spend your time reflect your personal and business goals and plan? What activities wasted your time? What choices are you making and are these choices getting you to where you want to be?

*Day*_____

Activity	7:00 AM				8:00 AM				9:00 AM				10:00 AM				11:00 AM				NOON			

1:00 PM	2:00 PM	3:00 PM	4:00 PM	5:00 PM	6:00 PM	Total Time

Day: Wednesday, August 9, 2000

Activity	7:00 AM				8:00 AM				9:00 AM				10:00 AM				11:00 AM				NOON			
Mail	▓																							
Scheduling		▓	▓																					
Bidding				▓	▓												▓	▓		▓				
Driving						▓	▓		▓	▓			▓	▓										
Visiting jobsites								▓	▓			▓	▓											
Return/phone															▓	▓			▓					
Handle problem																						▓		
Revu Financials																							▓	
▲																								
Poor time																								
management																								
Better time																								
management																								
▼																								
Mail	▓																							
Scheduling		▓	▓																					
Bidding				▓	▓	▓	▓	▓	▓															
Driving										▓	▓			▓		▓		▓						
Visiting jobsites												▓		▓			▓	▓						
Phone																					▓	▓	▓	
Handle problem																								
Revu Financials																								
Appt. w/myself																								

1:00 PM				2:00 PM				3:00 PM				4:00 PM				5:00 PM				6:00 PM				Total Time
																								.25 hours
													▓	▓										1 hour
					▓	▓						▓	▓											2.25 hours
							▓	▓			▓	▓												2.5 hours
									▓	▓	▓													1.75 hour
												▓												1 hours
																								.25 hours
▓																								.5 hours
																								.25 hours
									▓	▓														1 hour
																								1.75 hours
																								1.25 hours
																								1.5 hours
																								.75 hours
▓	▓	▓																						.75 hours
				▓	▓	▓																		.75 hours
								▓	▓	▓	▓													1 hour

Once you analyze exactly where you are spending your time, think about how you should and want to be allocating this precious possession and how you can do so more effectively. We will come back to time management with ideas and suggestions in the next chapter and throughout this book. First, there are a few things you need to do.

"TO DO" List

Managing Your Time #1

1. Write down your personal goals in your notebook.

   • *Be sure they are specific, measurable, and realistic.*

   • *Be sure they include professional as well as personal goals.*

2. Do the dreaded 15 minute time analysis for two weeks.

Chapter 3

TIME MANAGEMENT TECHNIQUES YOU CAN USE

*Life is like playing a violin solo in public
and learning the instrument as one goes along.*

— Samuel Butler

Your Brain And Your Perfect Week

The first thing you need to do is buy an appointment book. It must be a week-at-a-glance type. One day is not long enough to get things done. You have to start thinking of the week as a conceptual whole. You need to see the whole week to effectively plan what you are going to do and when. Get one that has plenty of space for writing things down. I really like the brand Quo Vadis and their Trinote Agenda Planning Diary style. You can purchase one at most office supply stores.

Stop thinking of your appointment book as an appointment book. Think of it as your **"BRAIN"**. Everything will go in it. I do mean *everything!* — appointments, directions, things you need to do, picking up the kids, the laundry, birthdays, and your plan of attack. Make it a habit to reach for your brain every time you agree to attend a meeting or think of an appointment you need to make. Pencil forward all deadlines. EVERYTHING goes in here — no more slips of paper on the floor of your truck, or a phone number you need left at your office. Have an appointment? Write down the directions and the phone number in your brain. Need to get back to a potential customer in a month? Pencil it where it goes. A friend tells you about a great book? Write it in your brain. Need to buy a tool, or drop something off? Into the brain it goes. Get the idea?

Now you are going to create your perfect week. First, make a copy of one of the blank weeks in your brain. Then think about how you would like your week to be. Are you sharpest in the morning? In the afternoon? Do you need to visit job sites? Go out and see customers? Do you have projects or bids that need quiet concentration? Are there times you need to be accessible to your staff? When do you have your weekly staff meetings? Need to get to the gym? With these types of considerations in mind, plot out your perfect week. (*Be sure to include an appointment with yourself. This is extremely important. I will discuss this idea more in the following example.*)

If you are a subcontractor, a perfect week might look like the example on the opposite page. Because you need to be accessible to your crews as they head out for the day, the early mornings would be spent on activities that can handle interruptions, such as the mail, signing checks, or reviewing invoices. So don't plan anything that requires concentrated, uninterrupted time. This might last from 7:30 to 8:30.

Once the crews are gone, for the next two hours each day, you close your door and create the uninterrupted time you need to do bids, projects, proposals, or whatever you do that requires peace and quiet. Excluding emergencies, you have your calls held, and ask not to be disturbed. From 8:30 to 10:30 you are otherwise unavailable.

Since you have been inaccessible for two hours, use 10:30 to 11:30 or 12:00 to catch-up. You can return and/or make calls, answer questions, or delegate tasks. Except on Tuesdays, that is when you have your management team meeting from 10:30 - 11:30.

You might schedule the time you spend out of the office from 1:00 to 3:00 or 3:30. On Mondays and Wednesdays you visit job sites. On Tuesdays and Thursdays you look at potential jobs and see clients. About now you are thinking "sure thing" (with the proper tone of sarcasm) or "no way will my customers fit this schedule."

Try this. Since you are now organized and you know how you want your week to go, you have an advantage. The customer calls and wants

A Perfect Week

Monday, August 4
7
8
9
10
11 Calls / Staff
12
1   Visit
2   job
3   sites
4
5 Return & make calls; available to staff; delegation
6

Time to be available to employees

Uninterrupted time for projects

Tuesday, August 5
7
8
9
10
11 Management team
12 meeting
1   See clients,
2   customers
3
4
6

Wednesday, August 6
7
8
9
10
11 Return & make
12 calls; delegate
1   Visit
2   job
3   sites
4   Weekly
5   employee
6   meeting

Thursday, August 7
7
8
9
10
11 Return & make calls; available to staff;
12 delegation
1   See clients,
2   customers
3
4   Misc. tasks
5
6

Time to be available to employees

Uninterrupted time for projects

Friday, August 8
7
8
9
10
11
12
1   Appointment
2   with myself
3
4   Golf
5
6

Saturday, August 9
7
8
9
10
11
12
1
2
3
4
5
6

you to look at a job. Instead of asking them when they want to meet (giving them control of the situation), you say, "I have some time on Tuesday or Thursday afternoon. Which works best for you?" Nine times out of ten one of these times will do. You are now in control of your calendar and time. Do this also with geography, so you are not running all over town. Say, "I will be in your area on Tuesday afternoon. Will that work for you?" Control your schedule and time, or someone else will be glad to do it for you.

When you get back to the office at 3:30, you will once again have to be accessible to people in the office and return phone calls. You also want to be accessible to the crews when they return. On Wednesday afternoon you have your weekly staff or field meeting. At the end of the day you close the door once more to review what you have accomplished and prepare for tomorrow. Thus goes a perfect week. Do I hear another sarcastic "sure thing?" Keep reading.

Some businesses or jobs are easier to plan than others. If you receive your work from others, or your job requires you to react to customer needs, structure your week more loosely. But, you can still structure it. The more you structure, the more control you will have. Give it a try. And then try it again. It *will* get better.

Once you create your perfect week, communicate it throughout your business. Enlist employees in making it work. Have them create their perfect week as well. Most likely, each person needs some uninterrupted time, but everyone cannot have it simultaneously. Coordinate people's efforts; take turns having uninterrupted time versus being number one on the phones or with customers.

To have your perfect week run smoothly, you must keep a weekly appointment with yourself no matter what. When things get busy, the tendency will be to give this time away. *Don't do it!* This is the time you need to get organized.

Here is what you do during this appointment. Close your door. Look over your company plan and your personal goals, and then go through your "brain". Come up with a list of things to do. Now using a simple system like A, B, C, or 1, 2, 3, rank items on the list. Then lay out your priorities within the template of your perfect week. For example, schedule time for that job proposal you need to write. Use some of your morning quiet time to prepare a performance review, and then schedule the time for the review in your brain. Need to meet a new client? Call for an appointment and schedule it into a time slot.

Remember, however, there are still only 1440 minutes in a day. You may find that before you get to the bottom of your list, you have run out of room in your week. It will then be time to delegate. Before we get to how to do that, one last reminder about the perfect week — this appointment with yourself to plan your work is critical to managing your time. **IF YOU DON'T PLAN YOUR TIME, SOMEONE ELSE WILL.**

Sometimes all hell breaks loose, and you just have to deal with it. Once the fire is out and the crisis is over, do not throw away all your good planning. Go back and replan the remainder of the week. If you had to deal with a crisis for three hours, three hours will not magically reappear in your week. Instead of working yourself sick, move three hours of work into next week. Find it, move it, and then get back into your planned workweek.

The key here is to stay focused on your priorities. By being organized in this way you can say "No" when you need to, or you can evaluate a new activity in relationship to what you have already laid out. You can also make changes or additions without working yourself to death. The key is not to prioritize your schedule but *to schedule your priorities.*

Yes, You Can Delegate!

Why don't you delegate? "Because I can do it easier myself." "If someone else does it, I may not have a job." "They won't get it right, and I'll have to do it again." "I don't have the time to train someone else." Sound familiar?

I am reminded of an owner who did all the paperwork for a government required inspection. When I asked him why his assistant wasn't doing this, he told me he didn't have time to train him. I asked how long the training would take. He said at least three hours. I asked how long the paperwork for each inspection took. He said about an hour. I asked how many he did a week. He said two to three. Together, we figured out that if he spent the time to train an employee, he would be time ahead in less than two weeks. Pick any job you could be delegating, and figure this one out for yourself!

Another reason owners and managers don't delegate is because the last thing they want is more responsibility. They think the same is true for their employees. However, employees — at least the good ones you will be hiring after you read this book — want more responsibility; they want to learn new things. What does that say about them? It says that they are valuable, important, and reliable. So honor them by delegating responsibility to them.

Most of the reasons people have for not delegating are gut level reasons which have nothing to do with the tasks or the people available. They will not delegate because they are afraid. They are afraid they will lose control, or fear others will make mistakes. Unfortunately, many owners lack delegating skills, and so when they do delegate, they often dump work without clear explanations. Naturally, the worst might happen. Here are some simple steps to learn how to successfully delegate.

- *Pick the right person for the job.*

For example, you want some uninterrupted time and don't want clients getting an answer machine. Choosing someone to cover your phone requires some subtle thought. Not everyone sounds good or has good telephone skills. When delegating, be sure the employee has the time and the aptitude, and that the new task fits in with the rest of their duties.

- *Be very clear about your expectations and have the employee repeat them back to you.*

Don't dump a job and run. Take the time up-front to clarify the details. You want a preliminary draft? Double spaced? Say so. Have the person repeat the instructions. This is for you! We are dealing with your comfort zones now. Say something like, "I am new to this delegation stuff, so for my comfort, please tell me what I need you to do. It has nothing to do with my trust in your ability. I just want to be sure I explained it clearly enough."

- *Be very clear about due dates. Determine benchmark dates for progress checks and write them in your "brain."*

This is critical. If this is the first time you are delegating this type of project, include more dates for progress checks. Both you and the person to whom you are delegating need to write these dates in their brains. You are only checking up and advising, not hovering or taking back. Be sure to follow up on these dates.

- *Secure their commitment and assure them of your faith in their ability to do the job.*

Don't assume they will do the job; ask. Tell your employees that you believe they are capable. Don't assume they know.

- *Let them do it their way; different does not mean wrong.*

This might be the toughest thing you will have to do. People approach projects differently. Since you have been clear with your expectations and have established follow-up dates, you should be free from disaster. Let them do it their way.

- *Don't do the job for them and avoid reverse delegation.*

Some people are great at giving back projects. Even if the employee is having a hard time, resist the urge to take it back. Instead, coach them, train them, support them, and if you have chosen the right person, they will learn it eventually.

- *Celebrate success.*

Once the job is complete, praise people. Let them know how much they helped you and how much you appreciate their work. This is one of the best tools in a supervisor's arsenal. It makes people want to do more for you. And it's free.

- *Delegate more complex tasks as your confidence grows.*

Give your people as much responsibility as they can handle. They'll love it, and so will you.

Is Procrastination Your Problem?

In my time management classes we brainstorm a list of time wasters. Procrastination always makes the list. The most important thing to remember about procrastination is that it has different causes at different times. So, before you can apply the right solution, you must first identify the cause. If you think you or an employee is procrastinating because of laziness, while in reality the problem is a lack of self-confidence, you will most certainly apply the wrong solution. Solve the right problem.

Common causes of procrastination and some solutions:

• *Being a Perfectionist*

Put a time limit on jobs; determine the final product parameters at the beginning and stick to the plan.

• *Fear*

Expose your fears to the light of day. Things are rarely as bad as you imagine them to be. Create worst-case scenarios to the point of absurdity. Look at what you need to get started. Create a plan and stick to it.

• *Inability to set priorities*

Go back to your values, your goals, and what the company needs. Set daily, weekly, and monthly goals. Make a list and do it.

• *Boredom*

Create rewards. Shift activities — a boring one followed by one you want to do. Do the boring task first. Set time limits for how long you have to stay focused on a task.

• *Overwhelming task*

Divide it into manageable chunks and then delegate parts of it. Distribute the rest throughout your day or week until the big job is done. Remember that life by the mile is a trial, life by the inch a cinch. Create inches.

• *Self confidence*

Take an honest look at yourself and your strengths. Appreciate your talents, abilities, and past successes. Make a list of your strengths as they relate to this job. Think and project a positive self-image.

• *Forgetfulness*

Write it down. Put in your appointment book what you need to do, whom you need to call, and where you need to be. Make this the starting place for planning your week. Make a plan and act. Keep lists.

• *Confusion*

If you are unclear about what is expected of you, ask for clarification until you have adequate information to move forward. If you are confused, there is no such thing as a stupid question.

Now that we have talked about managing your personal time, let's talk about managing your time in relationship to other people and things.

Making Your Meetings Work

If you do them right, meetings are an effective, cost-efficient management tool and great time savers. You can eliminate the frustrating nature of meetings by starting and ending them on time, giving them a clear purpose, and having excellent follow-through.

Here are a few ideas for running effective meetings.

• *Always start on time*

Even if only one other person is in the room, start the meeting. Do not go back over material already covered for someone coming in late. Talk with them later. Remember, you want to positively reinforce the behaviors you want, not the behaviors you don't want. Several companies I know charge people for every minute they are late or assign them an unpleasant chore, such as cleaning the break room — Very effective.

In one company the worst offender was the owner. So we figured out how much the meeting was costing the company per minute (all wages added up and divided by 60). This came to 25 cents a minute. We planned to charge the late people, in this case the boss, 25 cents per minute late, put the money in a jar and use it for a pizza feast. Unfortunately, our plan worked too well, and the boss never had to contribute to the kitty. The good news was that the meetings always started on time!

• *Always end your meetings on time.*

Honor people's other commitments. Do so by ending your meetings on time. If you don't, toward the end of your meetings, people will start to drift mentally, wondering how long you will run over this time. To prevent this drift, end on time.

• *Always use an agenda.*

An agenda ensures that you will cover all the important topics. In advance of the meeting, give people the opportunity to add to the agenda, and then distribute it at least one day before the meeting. This will encourage the flow of creative ideas, because your people will have the time to contemplate and incubate. This also avoids a problem I hate, which is being asked what I think without having the time to think about it. Give your people the opportunity to think about and be prepared for the meeting.

Set a time frame for each agenda item. On the sample agenda that follows, the time of each agenda item is in the left column. It's easier to track the meeting's progress by writing down the time as a clock reference — 9:00 to 9:20. Then you can let the time be the "bad guy." A lot of energy on a topic? You can say, "If we are going to finish on time, we need to move on." Or, you can ask people to meet before the next meeting to develop a report or recommendation, "because we need to cover other topics today and still end on time."

Lack of follow-through also causes frustration. That is what the three columns on the right side of the sample agenda address. When you hand out the agenda, these columns are blank. They are filled in as the meeting moves along. In the example, old business reflects what was recorded in the who/what/when columns at the prior meeting. In many meetings, I have seen someone come up with a good idea, but it is never assigned to anyone for follow-up. When you discuss an action item, be sure to fill in exactly *what* it is, *who* is going to do it, and *when* it will get done. At the following meeting be sure these items appear as "old business" in the "agenda" column. Write what it is and who was going to do it. By getting the agenda out the day before, even if the person forgot their commitment, they have 24 hours to get it done. Filling out the agenda form and the agenda itself work toward assuring good follow-through occurs.

Be sure to include a "Good Idea" agenda item. Your employees are full of great ideas, and you need to create a forum to draw them out. Follow-

Meeting Agenda

To: _____

Date: _____

TIME	AGENDA	WHAT	WHO	WHEN
9:00-9:20	**Old Business** Joe: *Results from phone survey* Mary: *update on employee benefits* **New Business**			
9:20-9:25	● *Time to do planning* *– Schedule when*			
9:25-9:35	● *Review financial statements*			
9:35-9:45	● *Personnel:* *New employee orientation procedure*			
9:45-9:50	● *Overtime issues*			
9:50-10:00	● *Other business* *– Good ideas* *– Celebrations*			

up on suggestions is critical. If you cannot implement a good idea, you still need to get back to the person who gave it. Say, "I looked into that good idea of yours. I cannot implement it now. (Give them a reason.) But thanks for the idea." Encouraging everyone to think about how things can be done better keeps you on the competitive edge.

Types of meetings

I recommend three types of meetings. The first is a management team meeting. The people who should attend are those who have broad responsibilities in the business and who are most effective when they understand the big picture. Agenda items would include: review of financial information, monitoring of the annual plan, personnel issues, review of upcoming work, status of sales, and marketing.

The grouping of staff or field meetings depends on your type of business. An administrator might have an office staff meeting, the superintendent one with the field personnel, or the store manager one with the sales staff. The agenda would include such things as useful information that comes out of a management team meeting, a status report on the progress of the annual plan, safety and training items, and solicitation of good ideas.

These two types of meetings should occur weekly and be paid time. If you have meetings every other week, you lose flow and continuity. One purpose of the meetings is to create and maintain a sense of teamwork and ownership. Overall, meetings help a business run smoothly and profitably by enhancing communication. That's why you should pay employees to be there. The meetings will, if done well, pay the company back by reducing misunderstandings, by reducing mistakes, and increasing productivity through improved communications.

The final meeting (And a very important one) is an "AM Huddle." This is a daily, five minute, stand-up, no donut, no coffee meeting of people whose jobs support each other. You come to this meeting with your "brain" in hand. You share what you are trying to accomplish that day, what assistance you need or can offer to others, and leave with an understanding of who will be where and what they need: whether it's support, help with errands, or to be left alone to get a project done. It is like an organized interruption that will reduce interruptions later on. It contributes to people's ability to support and assist each other. Try it. Even in the smallest company, it is a very effective use of time.

Making Telephone, Fax, and E-mail Work for You

A telephone — you can love it or hate it, but you have to have it. Here are a few ideas that you can use to create a more loving relationship with your phone.

• *Take and leave substantive messages*

Phone tag is a very boring game. Research shows that of all the calls made only 30% require that two people be in actual contact. This is why voice mail works. If someone is taking messages for you, be sure they get all the useful information. Have the message taker write down the following: the reason for the call, if a callback is necessary, the best time to return the call, and the number. In this way, when you are ready to make the return call you will have what you need in front of you.

If you use an answering machine, structure your answering machine message to elicit this information. If you are the one leaving a message with another person or on an answering machine, make sure you include all the above information as well.

• *Group your calls*

Make and return your calls in groups. Since you have done your "perfect week", you have included time to do this. Grouping your calls is very effective because you get on a roll with the calls. This is particularly powerful if you are making sales calls. The first one takes an enormous amount of energy. The subsequent ones flow. Also, do not interrupt yourself by making or receiving calls when you are working on a project or talking with your staff. I know it may be a nice distraction or more fun that way, but it is not most effective.

• *Getting off the phone*

Anyone ever experience an over-long caller? Control is the key here. Start your calls with a clear statement of the call's purpose. When finished, ask closing questions like: "Is there anything else you need?" "Is that all I can do for you now?" If the person is persistent, pretend someone just walked into your office and say, "Oh, goodness. Someone just came in that I have to talk to." Or have your secretary ring that you have another call, or fake a call waiting from Japan. If these things seem rude, stop and think about who is being rude here — you or the person who will not get off the phone? A suggestion from one of my classes, that I have to admit I've never used, but one worth passing on is this; while you are speaking, just hang up! Blame it on the darn phone system.

• *Use your staff to screen, route, and return calls.*

Be sure your staff always finds out who is calling before they transfer a call, and that they always tell you who is on the line. Then, if you are not ready to talk to the person, you can have your staff arrange a time for a callback. Also, since your staff is now taking substantive messages, you can often read a message and then have your staff respond for you. They can also initiate and handle certain calls for you. For example, if you only need factual information from a client, have your staff make the call. Lastly, to facilitate effective phone use, your staff should be familiar with your perfect week. That way, they can arrange for callbacks during times that are best for you.

• Faxing and E-mail

If the phone call is solely to communicate information that does not require an immediate response, use your fax machine or send an e-mail instead. One caution on e-mail, only seven percent of communication is verbal. Tone of voice and body language are not conveyed. So humor or sarcasm does not come across well in e-mail. I've had to unravel many an office tiff because of misconstrued e-mail messages. Keep it simple and to the point. If a message has any emotion attached to it, walk down the hall or pick up the phone.

Paper Handling

Try to handle paper once. Do it, delegate it, or dump it! If you think you have a problem with this, put a check mark on the corner every time you pick up a piece of paper. One woman I know had 22 check marks on a paper before she realized she had a problem. Another suggestion that came out of one of my classes (I give credit when due) is to

TODAY'S INTERRUPTIONS

Date _____

WHO	WHY	WHAT TO DO DIFFERENTLY

tear a piece of the paper off each time you pick it up. Now, how is that for a direct way to eliminate a problem?

Interrupt Interruptions

To eliminate interruptions, the first thing to do is to track them and create a data base. (Use the form on Page 37.) By seeing the interruptions in the aggregate, you will see who is interrupting and why. Then you can figure out what you need to do differently.

Be aware that many interruptions occur because our behavior either encourages them or at least does not *dis*courage them. Do people waltz in and ask you questions they could answer themselves with a little effort? By answering them, you are reinforcing this behavior and encouraging them not to think. Remember Pavlov's stimulus and response experiment with dogs? Fortunately, as a human you have an opportunity to choose your response to a stimulus. Stop the cycle of interruptions by asking yourself the nature of the requests. Is the interruption legitimate or lazy? It may be legit and shows you that the person needs training. Or it may be the person is being lazy, and you have a personnel problem. Which is it? Respond accordingly.

The *interruption analysis* form (page 37) may show you that only one or two people are the problem. Talk with them about it. I had one owner who stopped interrupting his office manager simply by giving her the form. He'd come out of his office, she'd hold up the form like holding garlic in front of a vampire, and he'd turn around and head back into his office and use his *communicator* form. (Page 39)

On the *communicator* form simply put the names of the people with whom you regularly interact. When you need to tell them something, resist the urge to interrupt them and yourself by writing it down on the communicator instead. (Unless you are dead in the water. That is a different situation). Most things can wait an hour or two. When you get three or more items on the list, ask the person to have a mini meeting with you — an organized interruption. By then they will probably have a few things on their list as well. A much better use of an interruption, don't you think?

Remember too, that by having your AM huddle, you have taken care of many interruptions already.

Communicator

Name	Name	Name

Name	Name	Name

Rearrange Your Office

Look at how you set up your office space. Does it invite interruptions? Is your desk facing the door, so people can catch your eye and take it for an invitation to come in? Do you need to move the coffee pot, so you are not in the flow of traffic? Can you get a pony wall to give you some privacy? Do you need to get rid of the chair, so people have nowhere to flop?

Are the things you use most within easy reach? Do you have good lighting? Florescent lights flicker on and off faster than can be consciously perceived, but your brain somehow picks it up. Consider putting an incandescent light over your workspace. It has eliminated headaches for some people.

Finally

I could go on and on with these time management tips. I suggest you take a time management class if one comes your way. In the meantime, I have one last idea to help you. Just say, "NO!" Not to the person but to the project. Remember you only have 1440 minutes in the day. Be sure to use them to get *you* where you want to be, *with* the people *you* want to be with, and have *yourself* some fun along the way. Try to live each day of your life as if it were your last — because one day you'll be right.

"TO DO" List

Managing Your Time #2

1. Buy an appointment book and begin using it.

2. Do your perfect week, including your appointment with yourself.

3. Begin delegating to your employees.

4. Use an agenda for all your meetings.

5. Do your AM huddles.

6. Rearrange your office.

7. Analyze your interruptions.

8. Use your communicator.

9. Find a time management class to take.

Chapter 4

UNDERSTANDING AND USING YOUR FINANCIAL INFORMATION

There is no such thing as job security any more.
The only security is your own sense of a self-worth
and your knowledge about how to earn a living.

— Bobby Stone

True Confessions

I need to begin this chapter with two confessions:

Confession #1 — I am not now nor will I ever be an accountant. Though I religiously balance my checkbook every month, I do so by adding or subtracting the difference between my balance and the banks. (Unless it is a really big number.) I figure it'll work out in the long run.

This chapter is not a lesson from Accounting 101. The goal of this chapter is to give you enough information and understanding about your numbers so that you know how and why they are important in managing your business. I want to give you enough understanding so that you can ask good questions and request additional information and training from your accountant. I want you to know what the numbers have to tell you and how to use them in your planning, your pricing, bidding, and your hiring decisions. These are things I know — how to use your numbers to manage. I will probably never understand double-entry bookkeeping, but I don't need to. That's why we have bookkeepers. God bless 'em.

42

Confession #2 — I have a complaint when it comes to some accountants and CPA's. I have been called in to consult with businesses in which the owner was paying top dollar to receive financial information on a monthly basis. Amazingly, when the numbers were screaming that the company was in trouble, the accounting firm never bothered to pick up the phone and say, "We need to talk about this, or you will be in bankruptcy soon." Yet all the while the accounting firm was turning out the monthly bill and expecting payment.

I think you should expect, indeed demand, more from your accountant than plugging in numbers, running reports, and sending bills. I believe that you should be in "partnership" with your accountant.

Choosing an Outside Accountant

When choosing an outside accountant, you need to decide whether or not you need all the horsepower that comes with a CPA. You need a CPA if you must have an audited financial statement for purposes such as bank loans, or if you have stockholders or partners who want an independent look at their investment in your business. An audited financial statement will cost you a lot and not buy you very much. (They start at about $3000.) Because of the cost, and the fact that the technology now exists via computers to produce accurate financial information within your company, many lenders no longer require an annual audit in their loan agreements. Check it out.

If you have to use a CPA, I suggest you find a solo practitioner or a small firm. You want to have one person who works with you and gets to know you and your business. Don't be shuffled around from one accountant to another in a large firm. Remember, you want to establish a "partnership" with an accountant.

Since computers and accounting software can now do most things inhouse that used to require a CPA or bookkeeping firm, you are looking for an accountant who can:

1. Design a management information system that gives you the information necessary to run your business.

2. Show you how to read and interpret your financial information and how to use it as a management tool.

3. Stay on top of your tax situation throughout the year.

4. Act as trainer, overseer, and general question answerer for you and your bookkeeper.

You want a "partner" who lets you know what financial information you need and what it tells you, and how you can use the information to make decisions. When I was learning this stuff, I would go back to my accountant/teacher/friend every week and say, "Can we go over that stuff about gross profit margin again?" Hang in there and keep asking questions until you truly understand.

I know there are accountants out there (with and without the "Certified Public" part of the title) who will do all these things for a reasonable price. My clients and I are very fortunate, because I can refer them to someone who does all this and more. You owe it to yourself to find one of these accountants and make him or her part of your team.

Why Your Numbers Are Important

When your company is small you can see what is going on, and it is relatively easy to stay in control. As your company grows, you have to organize yourself differently in order to continue to see what is happening. Because your business is constantly moving and changing, you need to be able to see the present, anticipate the future, and learn from the past. Your numbers on a daily, weekly, monthly, and yearly basis give you this ability. These numbers appear in a variety of formats and reports, and together they constitute what is known as a *management information system.* (I will cover part of this system now and the rest in Chapter 5.)

Your Management Information System

Your Balance Sheet

Your balance sheet will tell you how well you are doing with collections, about inventory turns, and inventory overhead. It can tell you how old your equipment is and even more. If I tried to explain it all here, you would fall asleep, get confused, close the book, or worse! To best learn and understand these things you need your balance sheet in front of you and someone beside you answering your questions. So make an appointment right now! With your balance sheet in hand, ask your accountant to teach you the following.

The balance sheet is a financial picture of your business at a given moment. It is divided into three parts:

1. *Assets* are what you *own.*

2. *Liabilities* are what you *owe,* and

3. *Capital* or net worth or equity (three names for the same thing), is the *difference* between the assets and liabilities. Capital consists of the *money you put in* to start the business, *plus* the accumulated *profits* since the business started, *less* any *losses* that have been incurred and *less* any *draws* you have taken — like *dividends* or other types of *distributions.*

Assets
There are three types of assets.

1. *Current Assets* can be easily liquidated (turned into cash). They include, besides cash, your accounts receivable (money that people owe you) and inventory.

2. *Fixed Assets* are equipment, property, plant, vehicles — anything that is a permanent part of the business.

3. *Other Assets* are those that don't go anywhere else, such as prepaid insurance, deposits, and payroll advances. It is also the place you record intangibles, such as goodwill and customer lists, and things you have to capitalize for tax purposes, such as start-up costs.

Liabilities
There are also three types of liabilities.

1. *Current Liabilities* are debts that you expect to pay within the next 12 months. They include accounts payable (money you owe), payroll withholdings, short-term notes, and the *current* portion of long-term installment loans, such as your mortgage for the year.

2. *Long-Term Liabilities* are debts payable over the long term, such as your mortgage.

THE SIMPLE COMPANY

Balance Sheet: August 7, 1997

ASSETS		LIABILITIES	
Current Assets			
Cash	5,000	Accounts Payable	2,500
Accounts Receivable	15,000	Notes Payable (equip/autos)	10,000
Inventory	2,500	TOTAL LIABILITIES	12,500
TOTAL CURRENT	22,500		

Fixed Assets		Capital	
Equipment	25,000	Common Stock	10,000
Autos & Trucks	25,000	Retained Earnings	13,800
TOTAL	50,000	Current Year Profit	6,200
Depreciation	(30,000)	TOTAL CAPITAL	30,000
NET FIXED ASSETS	20,000		
Total Assets	42,500	Total Liabs & Capital	42,500

3. *Loans Payable* are debts to you, your partners, or your shareholders. Yes, for a variety of reasons, people lend money to their own business. Lenders will consider these owner-loans part of the capital of the business. (The capital of a business is listed in a variety of ways. It depends on the legal structure of the business: sole proprietorship, general or limited partnership, or of various types of corporations. Ask you accountant about which category of business you should choose — each has tax ramifications.)

There are some overhead cash flow costs reflected on the balance sheet. These include the owner's draw if you are not a corporation. If you are a corporation, you are paid a salary and it will show up on the Profit and Loss Statement (P&L). Other overhead would be your loan and mortgage payments if you own rather than rent your building or the loan payments on your vehicles and equipment. Rent would show up on the P&L. (We'll discuss P&L's and the importance of grouping these expenses accurately a little later.)

So what does a balance sheet tell you? Here are just a few things.

Ratios

Ratios are a quick and easy way to evaluate how things are going with your business. These relationships vary in importance from industry to industry. Find out what yours should be from your accountant or trade association.

1. *Current ratio.* This is the relationship between current assets and current liabilities. The rule of thumb is that the current ratio should be no less that two assets to one liability (2:1). However, you need to consider how good the assets are. For example, how collectable are the receivables, and how salable is the inventory?

2. *Quick ratio.* This measures cash and accounts receivable against accounts payable, and tells creditors the likelihood of whether or not you can pay on time. The rule of thumb here is one to one, but again, the quality of the receivables is critical to the equation. If they are more than 90+ days past due, they may not be so good.

3. *The relationship between total debt and equity.* This tells how much money you have in the business (the equity) and how much money the creditors have in the business (total debt). This is the ratio that lenders use to decline loans. If the ratio is less than one equity to one debt, you can forget borrowing money on anything but a fully secured basis.

Now it is time to make that appointment with your accountant!

Your Profit and Loss Statement

Your Profit And Loss Statement (P&L), Income Statement, or Operating Statement are three names for the same thing.

Your P&L is a picture of your business *over a period of time.* You should be looking at this monthly. I have seen businesses who get them quarterly or less frequently. This is not good. Since the P&L tells you how you are doing, the more often you see it, the faster you will be able to spot potential problems or opportunities. It is hard to effectively respond to a problem that happened three months ago. Get your P&L monthly.

The P&L is divided into three sections: Income, Cost of Sales (or Costs of Goods Sold — COGS) and Expenses. These sections are laid out like this:

Income or Sales
- COGS/Cost of Sales (direct costs)
=Gross Profits
- Indirect, Fixed or Overhead Expenses
=P&L Net Profit (Income)

(It is important to note here that P&L Net Profit does not equal Total Net Profit. Total Net Profit = P&L Net Profit minus any other liabilities on your balance sheet. This is because there are different overhead expenses listed on the balance sheet than on the P&L.) A good P&L will have columns for the current month, year-to-date, the current month for last year, and the year-to-date for last year. A really good P&L will also show all the expenses as percentages of sales. In a small business, the year-to-date comparison information is important because monthly figures might be skewed due to an extra payroll item, insurance coming due, or some other factors.

The income portion of the P&L is straightforward. It lists all the income for the business. If you are on the accrual basis, income will be posted when it is billed and expenses listed when the bill arrives. If you are on a cash basis, income will be listed when the money crosses your palm and expenses posted when they're actually paid. How you do this depends on your business, the IRS, and other factors. Check with your accountant.

(Please be aware that to use your P&L as an effective management tool it is necessary to have your direct and overhead costs separated as indicated in the following explanation. Unfortunately, I have seen many P&L's that do not completely separate direct and overhead expenses.)

The cost of goods/cost of sales section of your P&L lists the expenses that directly relate to producing your income. These expenses are also called direct or variable (two names, same expenses) — direct, because they directly relate to producing the product or service, and variable, because they will vary depending on the volume of work you do. They include the materials, equipment costs (but not loan payments), tools, and the

PROFIT & LOSS STATEMENT

	THIS MONTH	YTD	THIS MONTH LAST YEAR	YTD LAST YEAR	YTD % CHANGE
SALES	$15,833	190,000	14,917	179,000	6.15
Cost of Sales					
Labor with overhead	2,500	30,000	2,292	27,500	9.09
Materials	2,083	25,000	2,000	24,000	4.17
Subcontracts	1,250	15,000	1,125	13,500	11.11
Other direct expenses	2,429	29,150	2,333	28,000	4.11
Total	8,262	9,9150	7,750	93,000	6.61
Gross Profit	7,571	90,850	7,167	86,000	5.64
Overhead Expenses					
Advertising	417	5000	333	4000	25.00
Auto & Truck	292	3500	292	3500	0.00
Depreciation	417	5000	417	5000	0.00
Health Insurance	42	500	38	450	11.11
Worker's Comp. Insurance	42	500	33	400	25.00
Liability Insurance	42	500	31	375	33.33
Interest	83	1,000	83	1,000	0.00
Legal & Professional	42	500	42	500	0.00
Licenses & Permits	8	100	8	100	0.00
Office Expenses	208	2,500	196	2,350	6.38
Office Rent	400	4,800	367	4,400	9.09
Repairs & Maintenance	167	2,000	150	1,800	11.11
Supplies	42	500	33	400	25.00
Travel	42	500	50	600	(16.67)
Meals & Entertainment	21	250	29	350	(28.57)
Telephone	125	1,500	121	1,450	3.45
Utilities	83	1000	79	950	5.26
Wages (office)	1,250	15,000	1,125	13,500	11.11
Wages (owner)	3,333	40,000	3,000	36,000	11.11
Total Expenses	7,056	84,650	6,427	77,125	9.76
Net Profit	515	6,200	740	8,875	(30.14)

equipment rental that relate directly to producing the product, service, or the job. They include labor and the labor burden of the employees who are also directly involved in producing the product or service. Examples of direct employee expenses are the laborer, apprentice, line worker, gardener, equipment operator, baker, salesclerk, cashier, etc. Some expenses can be partly overhead and partly direct, so you have to put parts of them in both places — for example, a person who waits on a customer half time and does your books the other half. The rule of thumb is: If you need it to do the job or make the sale, it is a direct cost.

The overhead or indirect or fixed costs (three names, same expenses) are expenses that will occur whether you sell any product or service or not. These include such things as rent, insurance, utilities, employees who do not directly contribute to producing the product or service — such as the receptionist, bookkeeper, secretary, administrative assistant, estimator, managers, and most likely you as the owner. Your overhead should be predictable. These expenses should stay about the same month after month.

Here is a hint. You can tell if you have direct expenses mixed in with your overhead expenses if your overhead fluctuates greatly from month to month. If this is the case, review how you have classified your expenses.

To place the various types of expenses correctly on your P&L is critical. Why? Well, as you look at the example (or your own P&L), you will see that the income/sales and the costs of sales/COGS (expenses) are listed on the top half. Cost of sales subtracted from income equals your gross profit. If you have direct expenses down in the overhead expenses, you will be subtracting fewer expenses from the income, which will make your gross profit *appear* to be bigger.

Understanding and Using The Gross Profit Margin To Manage Your Business

The single most important number in your P&L is your gross profit margin. This is a percentage that you get by dividing your income from sales into your gross profits:

gross profit ÷ income = gross profit margin (GPM)

If your gross profits are too high because all your direct costs are not accounted for on the top half of the P&L, your GPM will reflect a higher percentage than it actually is. So who cares? Well, if you divide the GPM into your overhead costs, you will determine your break-even income/ sales number, which is a handy thing to know.

overhead expenses ÷ GPM = break-even sales number

For example, if your GPM is 50% and your overhead is $100,000 you have to sell $200,000 worth of widgets to break even ($100,000 divided by 50% = $200,000). But, if you have your expenses in the wrong place (you have direct expenses on the bottom half of the P&L pretending they are overhead expenses) then your GPM is wrong. Let's say that your GPM is really 35%. When you divide the $100,000 in overhead by 35%, you get $285,714. Now you have to sell $285,714 to break even. Big difference! Get your calculator out and run these numbers.

Let me give you an example. You own a bakery. You are thinking about expanding into the space next door to include bagels in your product line. This expansion will increase your rent, an overhead expense, by $1000 a month. Can you afford to do it? You can figure it out by using our formula. Suppose you think your GPM is 60%. You divide the $1000 overhead cost by 0.60 and find that you have to increase sales by $1666.66 each month to pay for this increase in overhead. *No additional profit begins to accrue until you cover this amount!* You decide that you can sell this much extra bread, so you rent the space. BUT, you have your expenses spread wrong on your P&L. You have some of your direct costs in the overhead. When you get the P&L right, you discover that your GPM is really 35%. Now when you divide the increase in overhead by your GPM ($1000 divided by 0.35) you get a break-even sales number of $2857.15. This is a few more cookies to sell. This is one way businesses get into trouble.

One more example — You want to hire an estimator, which is an overhead cost. Including all the labor burden (taxes, workers' comp, benefits) this position will cost you $55,000. You have a GPM of 30%. By applying the formula ($55,000 divided by 0.30) you find that *just to pay for* the estimator your sales must increase by $183,333. There will be no contribution to your bottom line until after $183,333 has been sold.

You can see how knowing and using your GPM will help you to make decisions about your business. There is a dynamic relationship between your GPM, sales, and overhead. I think of them as a triangle.

GPM

Sales   Overhead

You have to make this triangle work if your business is to be viable.

Another point needs to be considered when determining your break-even point. This is the cash required to pay for the overhead items on your balance sheet. Go to your balance sheet and get the mortgage, vehicle, and equipment payments. If you are a sole proprietor or partnership, your draw will be on the balance sheet also. Get it as well. (Remember, I said we would get back to these numbers.) Add your draw and loan payments to the overhead expenses on the P&L, then divide by your *accurate* GPM to see if you can break even on a cash flow basis. This will give you your total break-even sales/income number for the business. If you want to make a profit, add the profit you want to make to your total overhead number and divide by the GPM. This will give you your break-even sales/income figure with your profit included. (Hang in there — examples follow.)

So what happens if you do the above and you come up with a sales figure you cannot reach? You have to tweak the triangle. You have two choices: raise your GPM or reduce your overhead. Play with these numbers until the triangle works. It is working when you have a realistic sales goal and a realistic overhead, at a GPM that keeps you competitive.

How do you raise the GPM? You either raise your prices or become more efficient in producing the product or service. Raising your price increases the gross profits, because you are subtracting your variable expenses from a larger income number. But your current market might not bear the increase. This means you might have to rethink your niche.

Becoming more efficient means you reduce the direct (variable) costs. Thus, your gross profits are higher, because you are subtracting smaller direct costs from your income. You can reduce expenses by applying what you are learning from this book. For example, hiring smart and training increases productivity, reduces costly mistakes and rework, and reduces accidents (reducing overtime and workers' comp costs). All are a decrease in direct labor costs. Also: good equipment maintenance procedures reduce repair costs, effective materials management and purchasing can reduce materials costs, and you can take all your discounts on your payables. These effective management practices will reduce your direct costs, which will raise your gross profit margin.

The other way to make your triangle work is to reduce your overhead. Do you really need that fancy office? Can you get by with a bookkeeping service rather than a full-time bookkeeper? Can you reduce the usage on your cellular phone and keep the monthly bills reasonable? Do you and your estimator really need those new trucks? Can your computer or phone system make it one more year? These are ways you can reduce your overhead and lower your break-even sales number.

Keep working with your triangle until it works! Let's practice this a bit. Get your calculator and your notebook. Here we go.

Problems to Solve

Problem #1

You own a retail shop. Your annual income is $750,000. Your direct costs are $390,000. Your overhead is $375,000. What is your GPM?

a. 35%   b. 43%   c. 48%   d. 51%

Answer: Income of $750,000 minus the direct costs of $390,000 equals a gross profit of $360,000. Divide the income of $750,000 into the gross profits of $360,000 to get a GPM of 48%.

Yes or No? Does your triangle work?

Answer: No. Divide your overhead of $375,000 by your GPM of 48% and it gives you a break-even number of $781,250, which is more than your current sales volume.

Question: What do you need to do to make it work?
        1. Increase income   2. Decrease direct costs
        3. Decrease overhead costs   4. All the above

Answer: #4

Question: What can you do to make your triangle work?

Possible Answers:

I. Raise the GPM by
    A. Raising prices. (Increasing income, but reducing demand.)
    B. Buying smarter. (Thus decreasing direct costs.)
    C. Shortening hours. (Thus decreasing direct costs; but this idea may reduce income)
    D. Scheduling staff more effectively. (Thus decreasing direct costs)
    E. Other ideas?

II. Reduce your overhead by
    A. Monitoring and reducing utility and phone costs.
    B. Reviewing all insurance coverage to be sure you are getting the best prices.
    C. Checking out using a bookkeeping service instead of an in-house staff person.
    D. Using temps for short-term staffing needs.
    E. Other ideas?

III. Increase income by
    A. Expanding hours. (But watch for increases in direct costs.)
    B. Having more "sales". (But watch for a decrease in your overall GPM!)
    C. Increasing advertising. (But watch increased overhead costs.)
    D. Evaluating product mix and niche.
    E. Other ideas?

Problem #2

You own a heating and cooling service and repair business. Your triangle currently works. Now you want to increase your profits for the year by $20,000 so you can contribute more to your retirement account. If you have a GPM of 49% how much more business do you have to do a year?

        a. $20,560   b. $33,781   c. $40,816   d. $51,110

Answer: Divide your increase in profit of $20,000 by your GPM of 0.49 to get a needed increase in sales of $40,816.

Question: What are your other options for reaching your profit goal besides increasing how much you sell?

1. You can decrease your overhead, so what was once spent on overhead now becomes profit.

2. You can decrease your direct expenses. This raises your GPM, which reduces the break-even income figure.

3. All the above

Answer: #3. All the above.

Are you starting to get a feel for how this works? Here is something very important to remember. *If you cannot make your triangle work, close the business before you get any deeper in debt.* I have seen business people who did not understand this principle work themselves right out of business and into bankruptcy. They were busy subcontractors working for the top builders. They were the busiest retail shop or copy center on the block. They were manufacturers with many contracts — all bid too low. In each case it was because the business did not understand its GPM and its relationship to overhead and sales. These businesses virtually bought their jobs and gave away their product or service. They lost money on each job they did, on each sale they made, and on each service they provided. They worked themselves right out of business.

Another example. You own a bakery. You want to give yourself a raise. The kids are starting college, and you need more income. You need $15,000 more a year. Your GPM is 35%. So you divide $15,000 by 0.35 and find you have to sell $42,857 more cookies, bagels, bread and muffins this year to cover your raise. Can you sell that much? If not, can you raise your GPM to 40%? Now you only have to sell $37,500 more. What will that do to your prices? Will people pay $1.50 for a muffin? If you can't raise the GPM because your buyers will not stand it, you might have to take just $10,000 more a year. $10,000 divided by 0.35 = $28, 571 in increased sales. This many extra bagel sales is manageable. So maybe your kids have to go to community college for the first year or get a part-time job. Be realistic with what your business can do for you. Wishing it were so, will not make it so. Think these things through on the front end, so you don't get into trouble down the road.

If you cannot get your triangle to work, at margins high enough to cover your overhead, at a sales volume you can sustain — quit! You don't own a business. You own a job. So get one that at least pays you well, and put your money in a CD or mutual fund.

Your Annual Budget

Now that you know how much you need to sell and at what margin, you can do your annual budget. You can think of this as the financial plan for the business. Begin thinking of the budget by thinking about the large annual numbers: income, direct expenses, gross profit, overhead expense, and net income.

Once you have made your triangle work, you will know these big numbers. The next step is to break them down by line item and month.

First, by line item — Usually direct labor and materials are a percentage of sales. Using a spreadsheet, plug in these numbers. (There are books and software packages out there that have these formats and reports. Check them out.) You know from your history what your overhead costs have been. Plug in those numbers. Now analyze your numbers. Do you need to give raises this year? Are material prices on the rise? Did you move to a larger office? Adjust these historical figures to reflect the current situation or anticipated future. Include in your budget all the loan payments or draws from your balance sheet.

Second, by month — On your spreadsheet you need a column for each month. Spread these big annual numbers over the whole year. You know from your history, that some months are great, others not so good. For instance, if you are in construction, January, February and March income will not look so good. If you are in retail, you know that your sales will be high in November and December. In any case, spread your annual income as realistically as possible over the 12 months. Spread your direct expenses across the months as they relate to sales volume. Also, remember that unless you have periodic large payments for items such as insurance and property taxes, your overhead expenses should not change much from month to month.

Now add up the income and the direct expenses. Subtract the direct expenses from the income to get your gross profits. Add up the overhead expenses and subtract them from the gross profits to get your net profit (or loss) month by month for the year. You will see that some months will show a profit. Other months might show a negative number or a loss. (See the example.)

The month with the largest cumulative deficit will tell you how much financial capital you must have to make your budget and plan work. This money can come from your own resources, from bank loans, or from lines of credit. A budget also shows when you will have surplus cash that can be saved or used to pay off loans.

A side note here — Since banks are interested in how you will pay them back, a budget is important. This type of financial planning impresses bankers. Want a loan or a line of credit? Increase your chances of getting them by using your budget to show the bank where and when they will get their money back. (This also helps to establish a line of credit when you don't need it, which is when the bank will consider giving it to you.) Take this budget, all your other financial information, and your annual plan to the bank. They will be impressed. Visit your banker regularly. The key here is *to establish a relationship with your banker.*

Back to the budget — Once you plug in all your numbers, you can see if you can actually make the profit you wanted for the year. When you get all this information spread out, look at it to be sure it is realistic. If not, keep working with it until it is. Keep your triangle in mind at all times.

Once your budget is complete, plug the information into your accounting system. Now you can compare how you are actually doing with what you say you want to do. There will be a column on your P&L showing you the budgeted numbers for the month and year-to-date. This is called a *variance report,* and it is a very useful financial tool. Examine in detail any line item that is plus or minus 5% from the plan. Find

CASH FLOW BUDGET

INCOME	ANNUAL	JAN	FEB	MAR	APR
Job income	573,500	31,250	40,000	40,000	49,000
Misc. income	3,000	250	250	250	250
TOTAL INCOME	576,500	31,500	40,250	40,250	49,250
Matls & supplies	88,262	6,348	6,926	6,926	7,541
Outside labor	2,638	190	207	207	225
Wages	161,154	11,591	12,645	12,645	13,769
Payroll tax	16,000	1,200	1,265	1,265	1,380
Insurance	19,242	1,416	1,523	1,523	1,638
Sublet work	46,970	3,378	3,686	3,686	4,013
Other direct costs	85,174	6,143	6,691	6,691	7,274
TOTAL VARIABLE EXP.	419,440	30,266	32,943	32,943	35,.840
Salaries	90,000	7,500	7,500	7,500	7,500
Rent	4,000	333	333	333	333
Telephone	3,269	235	257	257	279
Utilities	2,294	165	180	180	196
Office expenses	4,500	375	375	375	375
Advertising	500	0	0	125	0
Tools and supplies	500	42	42	42	42
Truck expenses	5,649	406	443	443	483
Maintenace and repair	1,200	100	100	100	100
Legal and accounting	9,500	500	500	500	4,000
Licenses/taxes/permits	1,000	0	0	250	0
Dues/publications	2,400	200	200	200	200
Insurance	4,800	142	142	1,142	442
Interest	1,500	125	125	125	125
Payroll taxes	500	42	42	42	42
Miscellaneous	9,000	750	750	750	750
TOTAL FIXED EXP.	140,612	10,915	10,989	12,364	14,867
Net Profit (Loss)	16,448	-9,681	-3,682	-5,057	-1,457
Credit line use		-9,681	-3,682	-5,057	-1,457
Accumulated cash flow		-9,681	-13,363	-18,420	-19,877

58

MAY	JUNE	JULY	AUG	SEPT	OCT	NOV	DEC
54,000.	60,000.	60,000.	59,250.	55,000.	45,000.	40,000.	40,000.
250.	250.	250.	250.	250.	250.	250.	250.
54,250.	60,250.	60,250.	59,500.	55,250.	45,250.	40,250.	40,250.
7,541.	8,465.	8,465.	9,119.	8,465.	6,156.	6,156.	6,154.
225.	253.	253.	273.	253.	184.	184.	184.
13,769.	15,455.	15,455.	16,649.	15,455.	11,240.	11,240.	11,241.
1,380.	1,546.	1,546.	1,665.	1,545.	1,124.	1,042.	1,042.
1,638.	1,810.	1,810.	1,932.	1,810.	1,380.	1,381.	1,381.
4,013.	4,505.	4,505.	4,853.	4,505.	3,276.	3276.	3,274.
7,274.	8,150.	8,150.	8,770.	8,150.	5,961.	5,960.	5,960.
35,840.	40,184.	40,184.	43,261.	40,183.	29,321.	29,239.	29,236.
7,500.	7,500.	7,500.	7,500.	7,500.	7,500.	7,500.	7,500.
333.	333.	333.	333.	334.	334.	334.	332.
279.	314.	314.	338.	314.	228.	228.	228.
196.	220.	220.	237.	220.	160.	160.	160.
375.	375.	375.	375.	375.	375.	375.	375.
0.	125.	125.	0.	0.	125.	0.	0.
42.	42.	42.	42.	42.	42.	40.	40.
483.	542.	542..	584.	542.	394.	394.	393.
100.	100.	100.	100.	100.	100.	100.	100.
500.	500.	500.	500.	500.	500.	500.	500.
0.	250.	0.	0.	250.	0.	0.	250.
200.	200.	200.	200.	200.	200.	200.	200.
442.	442.	442.	442.	442.	442.	140.	140.
125.	125.	125.	125.	125.	125.	125.	125.
42.	42.	42.	42.	42.	42.	40.	40.
750.	750.	750.	750.	750.	750.	750.	750.
11,367.	11,860.	11,610.	11,568.	11,736.	11,317.	10,886.	11,133.
7,043.	8,206.	8,456.	4,671.	3,331.	4,612.	125.	-119.
7,043.	8,206.	8,456.	4,671.	3,331.	4,612.	125.	-119.
-12,834.	-4,628.	3,828.	8,499.	11,830.	16,442.	16,567.	16,448.

out why there is a difference, and determine how it will affect the plan for the rest of the year.

For example, your material costs are 5% over your budget projections. Why? Did all those nickel, dime, and quarter increases finally catch up with you? Then you may need to raise prices to reflect those increases. Or is it that you did a big material order because you got a discount for doing so right now? In that case, there's no problem. The important thing is that you know the materials are up 5% and you are in a position to decide whether or not you need to do something about it. If you need to make a mid-course correction, decide what it is and what to do. This is why you need to look at your financial information monthly.

Monitor these numbers.

If your sales do not come in as planned, make adjustments as needed. Reduce direct expenses or make more sales calls. If you are not holding your needed GPM, figure out where the problem is. Did your material costs go up? Are you having a lot of repairs, returns, or callbacks? Is the worker you hired too expensive? Are you not pricing or bidding right?

What about your overhead? Is it higher than you thought? Did you forget the insurance premium went up? Did you add a new employee mid-year? If the figures aren't cooperating, don't get mad at the budget. Get smart, rework your numbers, and go forward.

Monitoring will point out weaknesses and strengths in your budgeting process, so you can do a better job next year. Remember, check out the books and software packages that have these formats and reports.

Your "TO DO" List for the Next Three Months

1. Find an accountant you can work with, and make him or her your "partner."

2. Work with your accountant until you understand what your financial reports have to tell you.

3. Develop an annual budget.

4. Develop your Overhead, Sales, and GPM triangle, and keep it in mind.

Chapter 5

CASH IS KING

When we fail to change, we fail.

— Frank A. Clark

You understand your numbers. Your triangle works, and you've done your budget. Your P&L shows you are making money and holding your margins. So how come you don't have any money? Welcome to the world of cash flow.

Sales Do Not Mean Money in Your Hand

It is very important to note that sales do not equal cash, and cash is what you need to stay in business. People are often tempted to take on a few big clients or shoot for that once-in-a-life-time big sale — and all you have to do is lower your GPM to get it. After all, the volume will make up the difference — right? Wrong! What happens is that the big sale will stretch your resources to the max. You will have to buy materials up-front and/or pay your employees to produce the product or provide the service. Meanwhile, the income from the job will be 30 days out. You'll stretch your line of credit and pay more interest on the money. Since you bid low to get it, you can't afford any big glitches, and it usually doesn't work that way. The already lower GPM just got lower. The customer is a little late on their payment, so you miss all your discounts. Suddenly, you are out of cash and out of business. The golden opportunity was not so golden after all.

Instead, adopt *this* sales mentality. Look at each potential job or sale in relationship to your overall income, sales goal, and the gross profit margin you need — particularly in relationship to your cash and capital reserves. *If you can't get your gross profit margin from a job, don't do it.* Before you go after it, look that gift horse in the mouth and be sure you really want it. Turning it down may mean you have to bid more jobs to meet your sales objective, but you will be able to meet your profit goal, *which is much more important.* You need to look at your business in terms of where the cash is coming from and when and where it is going out — which brings us to the cash flow projection.

Cash Flow Projections

A cash flow projection (see example, pg.64) will help you to make short-term, as well as daily decisions about where to spend your cash. It represents a period of time up to 13 weeks forward, depending on the business. It is a rolling projection. As one week drops off, you add a future week to replace it. You set it up like your budget, but it has more detail. It shows the *actual* income you expect to receive, when you expect to receive it, and the *actual* expenses you have incurred or will incur during the period. There is a column for each week, and the income and expenses are plugged into those columns.

Here you name names. In the income section, put the name of each income source, and then plug the dollar amount into the week you expect to get it. Do the same for your direct and overhead expenses. You put in the names of the vendors you have to pay, how much you have to pay them, and when you have to do it. Do not forget to plug in that big quarterly insurance payment and your payroll taxes. At the top of each column put the beginning cash balance in your bank account. At the bottom of the column put the ending balance, which becomes the beginning balance in the next column.

This will point out if you have enough money to cover your expenses each week. If not, it will give you time to figure out how you will cover them. Will you use your line of credit? Contact your vendors and ask for another week? Not buy that piece of equipment just yet? Pay the phone bill a week late?

The negative or positive number from the bottom of each weekly column goes to the top of the next weekly column as negative or positive cash. If negative, you must either borrow or shift expenses to get to

Cash Flow Projection

	Week One	Two	Three	Four	Five	Six	Seven	Eight
Cash forward		2850	3150	-1950	850	-2300	-3700	-3700
Income								
Jones	3000			4000				3000
Smith		2500		2500				2500
Albert	1500		300			2800		
Thomson					3000			2000
Frank	3500		2000		2500			
WEEK TOTALS	8000	2500	3000	8500	3000	2800	2500	7500
Expenses								
Materials	2000				3000			
Payroll		2000		2000		2000		2000
Payroll taxes			1600					
OWNER'S DRAW	*2500*		*2500*		*2500*		*2500*	
Estimated taxes			4000					
Subcontractors				3000				
Gas		200				200		
Utilities / Phone				550				550
Liability Ins.						2000		
Rent	650				650			
Supplies				150				
WEEK TOTALS	5150	2200	8100	5700	6150	4200	2500	2550
over / under	2850	3150	-1950	850	-2300	-3700	-3700	1250

zero at the bottom again. You hope there will be times when cash is accumulating. Look forward to when you will need that cash to pay down loans, grant bonuses, buy equipment, or save for upcoming expenses or slow months.

Update and review the cash flow projection weekly, shifting the figures around as money is produced or spent. This way, you can hustle the money when it is due, instead of a week later when it shows up on an aging report. If you see no income projected for a particular week, start making those sales calls! It also shows you when to save your precious cash, because you know when you will need it later. It gives you control over the critical cash flow part of your business.

A few examples of how cash flow works — or doesn't — might be useful. For the first example, let's say you own a gift shop. You do your Christmas buying in June and July, but you will not see the income from those purchases until November and December. You need to pay for product and overhead between July and December. With the help of your cash flow projection, you can regulate the use of your credit line or cash reserves until the Christmas income arrives.

For the second example, let's say you are a manufacturer or a building contractor. In either case, before you bill for the completed product, you buy the materials and pay the labor costs. So there's a gap — managing the gap, between the cash outlay to produce the product and the income to pay for it, is critical. This gap can ruin a business.

Businesses get in trouble when they use a current job's income to pay for a prior job's expenses. Then comes a break. There is no current job. Expenses from the last job are still unpaid, overhead costs continue, and there is no income in your future. The P&L looks profitable, but the cash is gone — and so is the business. The meaning of "cash is king" hits home.

Cash flow projections, along with your annual budget, help you determine when you need money and how much. There are two time frames within which a company borrows money: long-term and short-term. Growth is financed with long-term money, and it is usually paid back in installments (for example, property and equipment loans). Seasonal shortfalls are covered by short-term loans, which are paid back within the same year. Keep these two uses separate. Do not use short-term money for long-term needs. Short-term money is expensive and difficult to pay back within the specified time. Again, talk to your accountant.

Besides your Balance Sheet, P&L, annual budget, and cash flow projections, your management information system should include the following reports.

Aging Reports

Aging reports come in two types. One tracks the status of your accounts receivable (AR) and the other your accounts payable (AP). In both reports there are columns that show current purchases (AP) or sales (AR), those 30 days to 60 days past due, 60 to 90 days past due, and over 90 days past due. (See the examples.) In the AR aging report, list your customers along with the total amount due to you. In the AP report, list your vendors with the amounts you owe them. In either case, you should have nothing in the last two columns and little in the 30 to 60 day column. Most should be in the current column. If this is not the case, find out why. Who is paying attention to your collections? Clearly, if no one is collecting, you may have a hard time paying *your* bills.

Produce aging reports at least monthly, more frequently if money is tight.

Accounts Receivable Aging Report

Customer	Total	0-30 days	31-60 days	61-90 days	> 90 days
Smith Company	6000	1500	2000	1500	1000
Jones & Son	2000			1000	1000
MNM Construct'n	3000	3000			
BB Concrete	1500	500	1000		
Al's Tile	3500	500	1000	1000	1000
Total	16,000	5500	4000	3500	3000

Accounts Payable Aging Report

Vendor	Total	0-30 days	31-60 days	61-90 days	> 90 days
Phone Company	400	400			
Utility Company	200	200			
Materials Co.	1500	500	500	500	
Accountant	200		200		
Sam's Service	200				200
Total	2500	1100	700	500	200

Job/Product Costing

Whether you bid jobs or make a product, you need to have a constant fix on how your actual costs are stacking up against what you bid or expected the product or job to cost. On a big job you need to get a weekly, updated job costing report with three columns showing what was bid, what has been spent to date, and the percentage spent. A fourth column shows how far along the job is: the percentage completed. If the percentage spent is more than the percentage completed, you may be in trouble. (See sample job costing report, pg.68)

For example, you get the bid to lay tile in a large, four-story commercial building. It will take one week per floor. The direct costs on the bid were $100,000 ($25,000 a floor). After week one, your job costing shows your expenses were $50,000 or 50% of the bid. But the job is only 25% complete. That's okay, because you have already paid for all the materials for the whole job. So in week two, the expenses are at 70% and job completion is now 50%. Week three expenses are 85% and the work is 75% complete. By week four you are at 100% of expenses, and the job is 100% complete. Just right.

If the scenario had been 50% expense and 25% completion, and the materials were not the cause, you'd need to focus on and monitor this

Job Costing Report

	Project estimate	Actual to date	% spent	% complete	Balance left in est.
Labor	3000	2100	70%	63%	900
Materials	2500	2600	**104%**	98%	(100)
Subcontractors	1500	1900	**126%**	100%	(400)
Other direct exp.	2915	450	15%	75%	2465
Total	9915	7050	71%	84%	2865

job very closely. Otherwise, you might lose money, because you could end up with 125% expenses at 100% completion — and there would be no time to do anything about it.

On small, repeat jobs, you might do the report at the close of a job. It will show only the estimated amount, the actual costs, and the variance between the two. For example, you own a print shop. You have a 50% GPM goal. You think a standard business card order will cost $20 for materials and $20 for labor, for a total cost of $40. To meet your GPM goal you need a 100% markup, so you bid $80. But your job costing shows you that the materials actually cost $25. So your profit is really only $35, or a GPM of 43.7%. By doing the job costing you can easily see that your shop underbid this job. Since a 50% GPM makes your triangle work, job costing tells you to put your price up to $90 for business cards. Get your calculator out and run these numbers. Make sure you understand this example.

These reports will highlight your strengths and weaknesses in bidding and production capability and should help you to fine-tune both.

It is important to remember that job costing helps you compare the GPM on the bid or sale price with the actual GPM. If your actual GPM is lower than the bid or sale price, figure out why. Materials underbid? Labor figured low? Too many mistakes? The weather? If the actual GPM is higher than the bid, smile and be happy, but also figure out why.

Share the job and product costing reports with the employees who are doing the work, since they are the ones who can do something about problems. At a minimum, share how you bid the job, so your employees know what comprises a good job. Better yet, share all your financial information with employees. More about this in Chapter Seven: "Opening Your Books With Open Book Management."

In Summary

Your numbers tell you a great deal about your business. It is your job to understand what these numbers are telling you and to review them on a regular and timely basis. You need to understand and use at least the following:

1. **The Balance Sheet:** It shows you the current position of the company, what you owe, and what you own.

2. **The Profit and Loss Statement or Income Statement:** It shows you how you did for the current month and the year-to-date. If possible, it should show the corresponding period for the previous year.

3. **The Variance Report:** This is usually combined with the P&L. It shows you how you are doing in comparison with your budget forecast and the variance for the current period and year-to-date.

These reports should be prepared and reviewed by the middle of each month.

4. **The Annual Budget:** Produce this about two months before the start of the year. Include your projected sales, direct expenses, gross profits, overhead expenses, and net profit goals. An annual budget projects cash flow as well as profit and loss. The more people who have input into its development the better. Review it monthly through the variance report.

5. **The Cash Flow Projection:** This is your working document to chart income and outgo on a short-term basis. Review it at least weekly, sometimes daily.

6. **AR and AP Aging Reports:** These show what you owe, what is owed

to you, and for how long. You need to produce and review them at least monthly; weekly is better.

7. **Job Costing:** Do this for all jobs to show what you thought would happen (the bid or cost estimate) versus what did happen. It is an ongoing reality check.

In this era of computers and software, the cost of gathering and producing financial information is incredibly cheap and amazingly fast. Sophisticated techniques, unavailable to small businesses as recently as ten years ago, are now in common use. You need to be using them.

Finally, and I say this again because it's important, find an accountant you can work with and make him or her your "partner." Keep asking questions until you understand all the above and then ask to learn even more. Do not feel like a dummy if you don't get it at first. Not many people do. Keep reading and asking questions until it is absolutely clear. *When you can explain it to someone else, you are there.*

This chapter is to get you pointed in the right direction. Once you "get it", you will never view your business in the same way. Running your business, instead of the other way around, will become an actuality. You will have a lot more fun and be a lot more profitable.

Your "TO DO" List Forevermore:

1. Produce monthly balance sheets and P&L's.

2. Review your financial information, listen to what it is telling you and respond accordingly.

3. Produce weekly cash flow projections and aging reports.

4. Job cost religiously.

Chapter 6

PLANNING YOUR FUTURE

"Cheshire Puss," Alice began. "Would you tell me, please, which way I ought to go from here?"

"That depends a good deal on where you want to get to," said the cat.

"I don't much care where . . . ," said Alice.

"Then it doesn't matter which way you go," said the cat.

— Alice in Wonderland

Why You Need To Plan

While it is true that you will end up somewhere a year from now, will it be where you want to be? For a business, planning is the path out of Wonderland. Why?

1. Planning clarifies direction. Without it, different employees will have different views about the direction of your business, and then they end up going in all sorts of directions.

2. Planning encourages everyone who *agrees* on the plan to pull in the same direction.

3. Planning clarifies priorities and purposes. It helps to eliminate confusion, waste, and overlapping effort. So planning speeds up progress.

4. Planning saves time, money, reduces stress, and maximizes limited resources.

5. Because planning provides feedback on progress, it motivates everyone and creates opportunities for victories and celebrations — fun.

6. Finally, planning maximizes commitment and morale by tying personal goals, both yours and your employees', to company goals.

Simply put, planning gets you to where you want to be faster. Remember, I emphasized in the goal setting section that if you don't have goals, you will be helping others achieve theirs. By having your own plan, you engage other people's efforts in accomplishing *your* goals. By having a plan, you WILL be more successful. The rest of this chapter tells you how to go about it.

Before You Start Your Planning There Are a Few Things You Need To Do

1. What Do You Want From Your Business?

Review the goal setting section in the time management chapter. If you haven't done it, write down your personal goals before you go any further.

2. Develop Your Mission Statement

A mission statement is one or two sentences about who you are, what your company believes in, and how you want to achieve it. Will you provide the best and most creative engineering? The most drought resistant landscaping? The finest customer service? Be most environmentally sensitive? A promoter of communities? Committed to employee growth? You must figure out who you are, and then write it down.

To start, brainstorm a list of attributes that your business reflects, or you wish it did. Take this list of words and work with them until you get at the essence. Then formulate your mission. This will not be fast nor easy, but it will be your guide as you plan, as you hire, and as you and your people deal with the world. Let me give you a few examples of mission statements.

> *I design beautiful and imaginative outdoor environments for both commercial and residential properties that do not tax the Earth's natural resources.*

> — Steve French, Landscape Architect

This tells you what Steve does (outdoor landscaping), how he does it (beautifully and imaginatively), and what he believes in (not taxing the Earth's resources).

> *The Redwood Empire Association of Life Underwriters is a group of life insurance professionals who strongly believe that their job is not over when a policy is sold . . . it has just begun.*
>
> — Redwood Empire Association of Life Underwriters

This is a clear statement of a long-term, customer service focus.

> *The Monterey Bay Aquarium is a nonprofit organization. Our mission is to stimulate interests, increase knowledge and promote stewardship of Monterey Bay and the world's ocean environment through innovative exhibits, public education and scientific research.*
>
> — Monterey Bay Aquarium

This lets you know that the Monterey Bay Aquarium is much more than an aquarium or tourist attraction.

In addition to guiding your company, your mission statement is a message to your customer; it is a way to differentiate your business from your competition. You can put your mission statement on your letterhead, your business cards, and post it in your office. In this way, your customers will be able to compare your mission to your competitors. (If they even have one.) Thus, your mission helps to encourage your customers to buy from you. For example, because of my background in the nonprofit sector, hiring a company that supports community needs is very important to me and can be a deciding factor in my buying decision. Other people might focus on whether a business is long-standing, or one on the forefront of technology, or one with well-trained employees. Know who you are, and let your customers know it.

A mission statement is also a touchstone for your employees. At my nonprofit corporation, we were about independence and integration into the community for people with disabilities. If the landscape crew was heading to a job and needed to stop and get some irrigation parts, it would be most efficient for my staff to run in and get the parts. But we were not totally driven by efficiency. We had a higher mission of

73

integration and independence. Based on our mission, my staff would make the choice to take our disabled folks into the hardware store to give them the experience of buying the parts. It took a little longer for sure, but it supported our mission. I couldn't be with my employees all the time. I had to let them know what kind of company we were, so they could make the right decisions on a daily basis.

If your mission is to produce a quality product, then your employees will know to take the extra time to get it right. Is your focus customer service? Then your employees know their job includes delighting the customer. Are you about growth and learning? Then your employees will help you to identify training needs.

Is what you want to do congruent with your mission — who you are? Do you need to modify your mission statement? Do you need to look at your direction and plan? Again, let me emphasize that planning starts with who you are. Be sure you know, because your mission statement becomes your guide during the planning process.

3. Determine Your Competitive Position

Before you start planning, you also need to think about where you are in relationship to your customer base, your pricing, and your competition. This is called your *competitive position.*

First, you must determine if your customer base has a broad or a narrow focus. If you are broad based, everyone is your customer. For example, Ivory soap is broad based. Look at their ads — men, women, children — that about covers it. Lava soap on the other hand is narrow based. Their customer is the dirty, greasy mechanic. What about you? Are you trying to serve everyone or a specific market niche?

Next, consider how your customer base is tied to your prices. For example, Greyhound Bus Lines positions itself as an inexpensive and broad based transportation service. A limo service is expensive and caters to a narrow group of travelers. Between these positions, there are inexpensive but narrow focused transportation providers, such as airport shuttle services, and broad based but more expensive choices, such as taxicabs.

Where would you plug yourself in? Broad based and inexpensive? Do you do subdivisions or commercial buildings and close your customer on price? Do you sell groceries to everyone and have sale items and bargain prices? Are you a quick-print shop with basic services and lots of copy machines?

Or are you in a narrow niche and expensive? Are you a custom builder, building homes at a $500,000 minimum? Are you a boutique food store with fine wines, fancy condiments, and expensive sweets? Are you a first-class print shop with graphic artists, computer generated designs, and two-sided, four-color printing?

Finally, what are your competitors' positions? Do you know? Are you all in the same niche, no niche? Is there a niche available to move into? By looking over the field, you might find a good niche. For example, I just heard about a rural *delivery* service for animal feed and pet food. You call in what you need and it appears. It may cost a little more, but in an area with limited access to these products, the customer is willing to pay a little more — A narrow focus that costs more: A good competitive position.

Let me give you another example. I consulted for a small tile contractor in Northern California who was trying to do it all — commercial jobs, remodels, and new construction. He was broad based and trying to be least expensive. His business was running him ragged; he was trying to be everything to everybody. He would bid jobs like ripping out showers in falling down houses and then hauling things to the dump, while he was also trying to do expensive custom homes with imported tile and highly skilled tile setters. With this range of customers, he had a hard time hiring people with the multiple skill levels he needed. He also needed a wide variety of tools and vehicles, and he had to present himself and his company in a variety of ways. He couldn't get his profits right, because each niche had different requirements.

Even though the ratty showers always cost him money, he was afraid to let those small jobs go.

We worked together to figure out what he wanted, both on a personal and professional level. With this as the starting place, he repositioned himself to be more narrow based and higher priced. It wasn't easy for him, but he began to turn down the small messy jobs (via high bids) and focused his attention on extensive remodels and new homes.

He worked on developing relationships with those contractors who did the kind of homes he wanted to do. He joined and became active in the appropriate trade associations. Gradually, his work began to come as referrals from these groups instead of directly from homeowners, and he began to get the high-end repeat business he wanted.

To do fine quality tile work, he began to train his employees or hire to the skill level he needed. He raised his prices and improved his sales skills. He learned who his competition was and how to differentiate himself from them. He acknowledged that he wasn't the cheapest, and he knew why. He took the leap and decided upon a competitive position — narrow and high priced — and then, through the planning process, committed his time and resources to getting there. Now that he refuses to be everything to everyone, he is much more sane, successful, and profitable.

Think about your competitive position and where you would like to be. The planning process will show you how to get there.

4. Understanding Your Numbers

Before you can go on to your planning, you need to understand the GPM, sales, and overhead triangle. (Review Chapter 4.) Know how your triangle is working now, so you can make the changes that will make it better in the future. Your decisions about income goals, sales volume, and gross profit goals will drive the rest of the planning analysis.

5. Decide Who Will Participate in Your Planning Process

Since the planning process will involve reviewing where you are now and then looking at where you want to be and what it will take to get there, the more good minds you involve in the process the better. This is a very personal decision. Some people hold information close to the chest. Others freely share. Decide the level of inclusion that makes you comfortable. I have conducted planning sessions with just the owner and spouse, with the owner and key managers, and with the owner, managers, and key field personnel. In my nonprofit corporation, the whole Board of Directors and all my staff participated. We ended up with 30 people.

Who you invite will drive the logistics of the process; you need to decide whom you want or who needs to be involved. Who do you trust? Whose council do you seek? Who has good insight into your strengths and weaknesses? Who will keep you honest? Who will ask the hard questions and help to come up with realistic answers? Those are the people you need.

Your Planning Process

Step 1: Getting Ready

Set aside enough time. You will not just magically wake up one morning and decide today is the day. Set aside a whole day or several two to three-hour blocks of time. The actual amount of time you need will depend on how large your company is, how many people are involved, and, to some degree, the extent and complexity of the issues before you. If you can, choose a time near your year's end, so you can develop a comprehensive plan for the coming year.

In addition to setting aside the time, find a good place to work. There should be some wall space to tape up flip chart paper, enough room for the participants, comfortable chairs, and room to move around. For supplies you will need felt pens, flip chart paper, and masking tape. Plan to bring in some munchies and refreshments also.

Before you get started, tape six sheets of paper on the wall. Label one "W.O.T.S. UP" with the current date. *W.O.T.S.* stands for *W*eaknesses, *O*pportunities, *T*hreats and *S*trengths. Leave one sheet of paper blank. Label one "Weaknesses," one "Strengths," one "Opportunities" and the last one "Threats."

Determine who will be the facilitator/writer. This can be anyone in the group, or you may want to use an outside facilitator. The advantages of an *outsider* are:

1. Everyone in your planning group can fully participate, because no one has to be the facilitator.

2. The outside person can bring a unique and external viewpoint to the process.

3. The outsider can ask the hard questions and/or identify issues no one wants to address — the elephant in the room.

4. The facilitator can assist in assuring full participation by each person in the group.

5. The facilitator ensures that the meeting stays focused and on time.

If you do not use an outside facilitator, be sure that someone is paying attention to the process and ensuring that everyone is given an opportunity for input. You need a guardian of the process for it to work.

Begin by having the facilitator explain the process to the planning group. The facilitator also describes what the end result should look like. Next, the group will talk about and analyze the business as it exists today. Then the group will talk about where the company should be in a year. Finally, they formulate this information into goals. These goals are assigned to specific people, dated, and then incorporated into your meeting structure. Now let's look at how to do this.

Step 2: Do Your Situational Analysis (W.O.T.S. UP?)

Within this step, the group will discuss the status and use of your financial information.

To begin the situational analysis, obtain and write on the sheet of paper labeled "W.O.T.S. UP" your income/sales numbers. Next, put up your gross profits and gross profit margin. If you don't know what these are, write on the "Weaknesses" sheet: "Don't know GPM." Get the idea?

Now, depending on the answers to the following questions, you will be writing things on the "Strengths" sheet or the "Weaknesses" sheet. Do you get financial information in a timely manner? Yes is a strength; No is a weakness. Do you review it regularly? Do you use it to make decisions? Does everyone in the company understand the information? Are your margins good in relationship to your industry standards? Does your GPM, sales, and overhead triangle work? Get the information up on the appropriate sheet of paper.

Your income/sales do not exist in a vacuum. They are the result of many things working together (or not). Thus, once you get the sales and margin variables analyzed, then you must go on to analyze the other variables that allowed you to do that volume of work at those margins. In short, you must look at each of the variables that allowed you to do your volume of business. Some variables you need to consider and some questions to ask are:

- *Products or services*: What are they? What percentage of total volume? What GPM for each?

- *Employees:* Who are they? What are their skills, strengths, and weaknesses? What is the level of turnover, and what is the employee availability in the marketplace?

- *Management:* Who are they? What are their skills, education, strengths, weaknesses, and experience?

- *Facilities:* Adequacy, upkeep, location?

- *Equipment:* New, used, old, reliable, adequate?

- *Maintenance:* Are procedures in place? Adequate, implemented?

- *Quality and dependability:* Of your product, service, staff?

- *Geographic base:* How far do you have to travel to get your sales/ work?

- *Resources:* Are the resources you need readily available?

- *Procedures:* Do you have procedures in place as needed? Which ones do not exist?

- *Organization:* Are you organized to be most efficient and profitable? Do you have job descriptions? Do you do performance reviews? Run effective meetings?

- *Economy:* What impact does the economy have on you?

- *Markets and Competition:* Where are your markets, and who is your competition? List them. Do you know how and why you are different? List your differences.

- *Advertising:* What are you doing and how well is it doing for you?

- *Finance and Credit lines:* Do you have a line of credit? Is it to the max? How do you use it? If not, do you need one? How is your relationship with your bank?

- *Training:* Do you do it, and is it effective? Do you need to do more?

- *Reputation:* Is it good?

- *Leadership:* How are you doing?

- *Government Regulations:* Are they a threat or an opportunity?

You are taking a "snapshot" of your business as it exists *right now*. You will describe, discuss, and dissect each of these variables. Write this information up on the W.O.T.S. UP sheet. Then for each variable, ask whether it is a Strength or Weakness. Does it represent an Opportunity or a Threat? Write this up on the appropriate sheet of paper.

Be thorough. Be hard on yourself. Be honest. The better analysis you do, the better the final product. Hang in there. Do not quit too soon.

For example, the situational analysis might look like this:

To do your $1 million in sales, it took three office employees and eight people in the field or production line and you. Two of the office people are strengths, but one is underutilized and in need of training — a weakness. All the frontline employees are a strength, but you have highly paid people doing the work of a laborer — a weakness. You have job descriptions written — a strength, but you have not gone over them with your employees — a weakness. You don't do annual performance reviews — a weakness.

The equipment you have to do this volume of work includes a computer system and software. The hardware is new and has plenty of memory — a strength, but your software does not integrate your accounting information with your job costing — a weakness. You have six trucks. Four are new or nearly new — a strength. Two are close to death — a weakness. Your equipment is adequate for the volume of work you do — a strength, but ongoing maintenance and tracking are poorly managed — a weakness.

There is a new competitor in town moving into your current niche — a threat. But growth in the area and the need for your product is booming — an opportunity. This new competitor is aggressively going after your customer base — a threat, but you have never really advertised to get work — an opportunity. You don't really know how you are different from this new competitor — a weakness. However, you have joined your local trade association and are learning more about your industry and who is in it — an opportunity and a strength.

Your paper on the wall might look like the example on page 82.

If you are doing this in two segments of time, this is a good time to stop. Looking at where you are now is enough for one sitting. If you are doing this in one day, it is now time for lunch and a walk around the block.

When you come back, you will take a look into the future. For most companies a one year outlook works. You may want to dream beyond that, but it is very hard to stay specific.

Picture yourself sitting in a planning session a year from now. What is your gross income/sales? What is your GPM? Your net profit? Your net profit margin? Just as before, what you predict here will drive the analysis of all the other variables. You are now going to analyze these variables in relationship to what you think your sales will be and what margins you want to hold.

Want to have higher gross and net profits, but you don't want to increase sales? Then you may find your analysis focusing on how to create more highly skilled and productive employees. (Hire better, and train more.) It may focus on better bidding or changing your competitive position. It may mean increasing your office personnel, so you can get out more to schmooze and market and bid.

You want to increase sales and hold margins? How will that decision affect the number and type of employees you have? Are the people you need available in the marketplace, or will you have to train them? Do you have enough equipment? Do you have adequate space to handle the increased volume? Will this affect who your competition is and how they view you and position themselves in relationship to you?

The decisions you make about where you want your volume and margin — i.e., your business — to be, will affect all the other variables, whether you think about them or not. So, it is better to plan for, anticipate, and mitigate the impact, rather than run into problems full steam with no plan

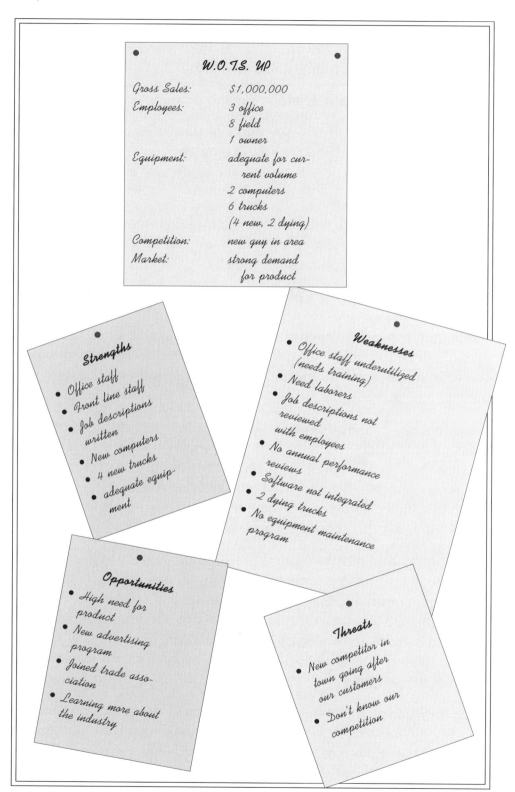

W.O.T.S. UP

Gross Sales:	$1,000,000
Employees:	3 office
	8 field
	1 owner
Equipment:	adequate for current volume
	2 computers
	6 trucks
	(4 new, 2 dying)
Competition:	new guy in area
Market:	strong demand for product

Strengths

- Office staff
- Front line staff
- Job descriptions written
- New computers
- 4 new trucks
- adequate equipment

Weaknesses

- Office staff underutilized (needs training)
- Need laborers
- Job descriptions not reviewed with employees
- No annual performance reviews
- Software not integrated
- 2 dying trucks
- No equipment maintenance program

Opportunities

- High need for product
- New advertising program
- Joined trade association
- Learning more about the industry

Threats

- New competitor in town going after our customers
- Don't know our competition

to deal with them. This is being proactive instead of reactive.

This is also the difference between having headaches and having fun.

So go through all the variables again; this time consider what you need to do to achieve your projected volume of sales at the desired margins. Once you complete this, you are finished with the situational analysis. Good Job! Quit for the day.

Step 3: Create Your Specific Goals, Assign, And Date Them

Type up all your information. You will usually be able to categorize the items on the lists into personnel issues, finance issues, equipment, and so forth.

Now you are going to turn the W.O.T.S. UP analysis into specific goals. Get with one or two people from the planning group, and from the information generated in the situational analysis, write up goals to address the strengths, weaknesses, opportunities, and threats that came out of the analysis.

Then assign each goal to a specific person or persons. Push the responsibility for achieving goals throughout the company — both to keep you sane and to increase understanding and buy-in of the plan. (Review delegation, page 27 and the purpose of planning, page 71) Then put each goal in a time frame. For example, in the financial area, your goals might be:

Prepare annual budget

> Who: owner with input from management
> When: one month before year end

Prepare financial information as follows: Balance sheet, P&L

> Who: bookkeeper
> When: monthly

Review financial information every month

> Who: owner and management team
> When: monthly

If the list included personnel issues your goals might be:

Develop job descriptions company wide

> Who: owner and managers
> When: by January 30

Conduct regular performance reviews

> Who: owner for management staff
> When: by February 15
> Who: managers for field employees
> When: by March 15

Write up and assign the goals first. Then go back and put in the dates. Until you establish all the goals, it is difficult to know what needs to be done first. Once dates are assigned, list the goals in two ways: once by person with the completion date and once by date. You will have a dated, chronological master list of everything you require to achieve your plan; and each person has a list, so they know what they need to do and by when.

About this time people start to get overwhelmed. You will tend to want to do everything in the first three months. This is when I start whispering in my client's ear, "This is an annual plan. That means that it will take a year to do it all." Since I am not there to whisper in your ear, you will just have to remind yourself; "This is an annual plan. That means that it will take a year to do it all." Otherwise, you will drive yourself and everyone around you crazy, and that is not the purpose here. So, "This is an annual plan. That means that it will take a year to do it all."

Step 4: Incorporate Your Goals Into Your Daily Activity

Include your time-framed goals as a regular agenda item for your management team and employee meetings. This keeps everyone focused on what you need to do to accomplish your plan. If you don't meet a goal by the recorded date, reevaluate it. Have things changed? Did other things become a priority? Is this still important? If so, move the goal forward. By regularly reviewing the progress on your goals, you will more likely end up where you want to go. Plus, as you check off one goal after another, you have lots of great excuses for celebrations.

A Real Life Example of Why You Should Plan

I was consulting for a very successful confined-space drilling and excavating company. There were ten employees, and the business contracted for work primarily in the residential market. By expanding into the commercial market, the owner hoped to increase his sales by 50%. Because of the niche and the economy, this was a realistic goal. After we did the W.O.T.S. UP situational analysis, we found four major areas to address in order to accomplish this goal.

First, the owner needed to build a management team. At that time, the owner had his hands in and on everything; it was his nature. The projected growth would make this impossible. He would be spending more time bidding and doing the other tasks on the owner's job description versus spending time in the field. (See owner's job description, page 7.) He would have to learn how to work effectively through and with his people instead of doing so much himself. Accordingly, he needed to increase employee responsibility in both operations and administration by formalizing the jobs of operations manager and office manager. This was totally feasible with the people already in place. He also realized that since he wanted employees to take more responsibility that he had to learn how and be willing to delegate.

Second, the field personnel that he needed to do the increased workload were not readily available in the marketplace. So he would need to start hiring smarter, develop a training program, and do more internal training to "grow his own" work force. Again, quite within reach.

Third, he would have to deal with equipment issues. The company used its current equipment at 75% capacity; thus, no new equipment was required. However, the company's growth would increase the equipment use to 90% capacity. He would have to design more effective equipment maintenance programs and increase the efficiency of equipment use. Again, totally feasible.

Finally, expansion into the commercial market niche would not sustain as high a margin as the current residential niche. The increase in sales volume did not translate to the same increase in gross profits because of the lower GPM. Nor would there be an equal increase in net profits because of the added overhead from the increase in management staff. There would be an increase in the bottom line, just not proportional to the volume of growth.

The owner looked at what it was going to take to grow his business and what he would get back for his effort. After doing the planning, he decided to keep his successful and profitable business just as it was. He promoted one of his managers to run the business, bought 1500 acres in Montana, moved there, and stays in touch by telephone and occasional trips to the business. The business continues to be successful and provides him with an excellent income, while he happily raises cows and rides the range.

The planning process makes you look hard at where you want to go and what it will take to get there. Then you can decide if you are willing to make the necessary changes to get there. I have worked with many businesses that have decided to stay the same size or get smaller. They created instead a more profitable, sane, and fun place to work. Others want to be bigger and more profitable. *The decision can be yours (if you choose to make it yours) by doing your planning.* Otherwise, like Alice in Wonderland, you will be somewhere, sometime in the future. Whether it serves your needs, desires, wishes, and dreams, is another question.

Make the most of your limited time and energy. Do your planning this and every year. Build in the time for fun, family, and fortunes! Build the business of your dreams.

> *If you don't know where you are going, you might end up where you're headed.*
>
> — Dr. Rod Gilbert

"TO DO" List

Your Plan for Planning

1. If you haven't done your personal goals yet, do them now.

· What do you want?

2. Do a mission statement.

· Who are you? Write it down and share it with your people.

3. Determine your competitive position.

· What is your niche? Broad or narrow? Cost based or differentiated?
· Why?
· Who is your competition? Make a list.

4. Lay out your planning process.

· Who?
· When?
· Where?

5. Do your W.O.T.S. UP situational analysis.

· Where are you now?
· Where are you going?

6. Create your goals, assignments and time frame.

· Who does what?
· When?

7. Monitor the completion of your goals through regular meetings.

· How are you doing?

8. Celebrate your successes.

· Party time!

9. Do your planning again next year and all the years after.

· It just keeps getting better.

Chapter 7

OPENING YOUR BOOKS WITH OPEN BOOK MANAGEMENT

It isn't that they can't see the solution. It is that they can't see the problem.

— Grover Cleveland

An Overview: Is This for You?

Open book management, in my mind, is the last, great management trend. You might have heard about management by objective, reengineering, total quality management, and teams. Each of these ideas contributes to the good management of people and processes. However, they are about *how* to do something. Open book management is about *why* to do something. It is about people learning to manage themselves, and it's about people making better decisions, because they have all the information, knowledge, and understanding they need to do so. They know why they are doing what they are doing.

Why do I think this is the last trend? Because, where else is there to go once you have embraced, empowered, educated, entrusted, and given a stake to your people? New techniques will surely be found, and there will be new ideas on how to do things. But as far as trends go, we have finally arrived at the bottom line, the underlying why — it's knowledgeable people who make the difference.

What is open book management? First, it is what the name implies — opening the books. Yes, this means showing everyone in the company your financial information: your balance sheet, your P&L, how much you and the company made last year or this month. Scary thought, huh? This will push you through some more of those comfort zones.

What will your employees think when they see how much you make? Undoubtedly, most of them think you make more than you do. Why is that? Because they see, for example, you billing at $100 an hour and only paying them $20 an hour. Or doing a 100% markup on your products and paying them $8.00 an hour. What they don't see, don't understand is how much it costs for the yellow page ads, the utilities, or the payroll burden. Not because they are stupid, but because they have had no reason to know, no way to know, and no one has ever told them it was important to know!

Try this. For several of the different hourly wages you pay, add up the hourly cost, the FICA, the worker's comp, the SDI, the SUI, the Medicare, and your health insurance, vacation, and any other benefit costs. Now share this information with your employees. We did this recently in a construction company. It blew the guys away.

The employees were astonished to learn that if their pay was $12.00 an hour or $23,000 a year, it actually cost the company $16.10 an hour or $30,000 a year. At $18.00 an hour or about $34,000 a year, the true cost was $23.38 an hour or about $44,000 a year. Amazingly, they didn't have any idea of the cost of disability insurance, or that the company matches their social security. They had even less of an idea about overhead, cost-of-sales, and all the rest. Why should they? Until recently, owners didn't tell them. This has to change.

In the early part of this century, a successful business did not need an informed, intelligent work force. Most products were standardized. One size fits all. Henry Ford said that the consumer could have any color of car they wanted as long as it was black — and he meant it! Jobs were specialized. Workers were replaceable cogs in the machine. The assembly line was designed to simplify the job and reduce thinking to a minimum. Indeed, workers were told not to think. That was the job of the supervisor. Layers of management and bureaucracy flourished. Companies ran in this manner were profitable. Change was slow.

Starting in the 1970's, we began to hear about global competition. The computer with its instant access to information arrived. Today, the consumer is king. We want individualized attention, products and services. The rate of change is escalating daily. A workplace with uninformed workers, waiting to be told by supervisors what to do and how to think, with layers of management approval needed to make decisions, will no longer be competitive. Now, the company that will survive is the one most nimble in meeting changing customer demands and the rapid changes in the marketplace.

What companies need now are educated and informed workers who understand business.

Open book management is about teaching every employee in the company about the competition, the marketplace, and where the money comes from and where it goes. It is about teaching them how the company makes a profit. How they, not the owner, have the ultimate control over how much money they make and how profitable the company will be, because the decisions they make every minute of every day have an impact on the bottom line.

Open book management is also about giving everyone a stake in the success of a company. What is at stake is sharing the profits if there are profits, and biting the bullet together if there aren't any.

Open book management is about creating a business of business people. It is about creating an environment where employees think and feel like owners.

I believe the companies that will thrive in the 21st century will be the ones that embrace open book management. This is not an easy process, nor is it a quick transition. But it is essential. Additionally, as responsibility for success is shared throughout the company, it will make your job easier and more enjoyable. So here's how to do it.

Resources Available to You

The first book you should read is *Open Book Management* by John Case. He gives a great overview. If you want a sneak preview of the book, Case published two articles about open book management in the June 1995 issue of *Inc. Magazine.*

The other essential book is *The Great Game of Business* by Jack Stack, the mighty founder of the open book management philosophy. It is the story of Springfield Remanufacturing Company's open book management program. I suggest you read Case's book first, because I find it helpful to understand the concept before reading about how one company implemented the process.

Spreading the word about open book management has led to a whole new division at Springfield Remanufacturing — the Great Game of Business division. They now have various videos, coaches, and a newsletter to spread the word. They host an annual "Gathering of the Games" conference. They also hold regional conferences where people who want to implement or who are implementing open book management gather to share ideas and resources. (You can reach the Great Game of Business at 3055 East Division, Springfield, MO 65802, phone: 1-800 386-2752, fax: 417-831-4260.)

As the word on open book management spreads, no doubt there will be more books, seminars and trainings available. In many areas in the country, networks have sprung up in which groups of businesses meet regularly to share what is working or not in their efforts to implement open book management. Business by business, they are learning as they go. This "grass-roots" phenomenon is one of the most exciting things about open book management. So go ahead, take another leap.

How You Get Started and How You Do It

First, let's understand the commitment. Open book management is not something you do today and then forget tomorrow. Employees have seen many a management craze come and go. Indeed, many will view open book management with some serious skepticism. From getting the gleam in your eye to having open book management fully implemented in your business will take up to a year, and then it will be an ongoing process that will require time and attention. Learn all you can about it before you start. Read the books; talk to people. This chapter will hopefully get you excited enough to check it out and get you pointed in the right direction. But, it is just the beginning.

Now let's understand the process. Open book management is not necessarily a change in your organizational structure. There are still bosses, managers, job descriptions, and performance reviews. It is more a change in how everyone thinks and acts than how you structure the company.

Open book management is about educating people to understand how your business operates and how it makes money. Once people understand the financial aspects of the business, then they can take responsibility for saving or making money. You do this with "games."

A *game* is a program you implement in order to impact one or more of your financial numbers in a way beneficial to profitability. Be sure that the game does not pit one employee against another. Design it so that by working together, people can make a difference.

Like any game, you must have a way to keep *score*. The scoring must be understood, visible, and tracked. You can post the scores by putting up scoreboards like charts, graphs, pie charts, or financial reports.

The savings or increased revenues from a game contribute to the money available for bonuses or profit sharing. Thus, people have a *stake* in winning the game, and winning should affect the bottom-line success of the business. The stake must be understandable, specific, highly visible, attainable, and *fiscally responsible*.

Here are three real life examples.

1. In a mail order company, the distribution center (where merchandise is packaged and shipped) created a game to reduce shipping costs. They realized that packages under two pounds were cheaper to ship by way of the post office rather than through their current carrier. By weighing and rerouting these packages, they were able to save $10,000 a month. A second idea was to reduce the number of different shipping boxes they used. They went from 17 different sizes to seven, an additional $10,000 savings over three months. Overall savings were posted weekly (the score). These savings contributed to the company making its quarterly profit goal — and more important — first quarter bonuses were distributed to all employees (the stake).

2. In a plumbing, heating and cooling service company, the game had to do with reducing shop time. (The time service technicians were paid when they were not making a service call.) It was an expense without an income. The reduction in this time took everyone's effort

— dispatch for effective scheduling, the warehouse to assure the trucks were stocked and materials were available, the technicians for calling in when they were leaving a job, and so on. Since the company's budget and sales projections did not project a large profit, profit sharing was not a likely option. But shop time was a large, direct expense item in the budget, so the *stake* in the game was sharing any and all savings in this one line item equally among employees. The *scoring* was done via a bar chart posted weekly. The game resulted in decreased shop time, which increased billable hours and thus increased profits.

3. In a retail shop, they wanted to track how their customers heard about them, so they could evaluate their advertising dollars. They had a coding system at the point of purchase, but the salesclerks would either not remember to ask the customer for the information, or just not code it in the register. A game was created to fix the problem. When 95% of the transactions for that week included the code, Lotto tickets were distributed. (One employee won $200.) The game continued until coding was a habit. Then a new game was developed to focus on another important goal: hitting monthly sales goals.

In each of these examples the employees were educated about why the cost savings, the time saved, or the codes were important. They went from only knowing that they *had* to do something to knowing *why* and the benefit of the changes. It was knowing the *why* that created the buy-in. Also, each game had a way to keep score and each game had a way to win.

Once a game has solved a particular problem, it has served its purpose. Then you move on to another "small" game. Small games impact specific needs. A way to identify the need for a small game is to think about what drives you crazy. Direct the big games at what keeps you up at night. However, you want to always tie any and all games back to the "great" game of company profitability.

Creating games takes some thought and effort. Before you can start open book management you must do the proper ground work. First, you *have* to do your planning and cash flow budgeting. (See Chapters 5 & 6.) Otherwise, you won't know:

1. Where to focus your games.

2. If there will be any profits to share.

3. How to give your employees the big picture.

4. How to set up a game that doesn't give away more than you have available. (Remember capital needs and equity.)

Starting a game and then realizing it could make you go broke can happen. Saying, "Whoops we have to start over," does not engender trust with your employees nor reduce their initial skepticism. So go slowly and start with your budget and planning.

Meanwhile, start the education process, because it will take some time. The end goal is to have people understand balance sheets, profit and loss statements, cash flow, equity, how profit is made, and what they can do to move the numbers one way or another.

They also need to know the "critical" number. This is a key number that gives you the daily or weekly pulse of your business. Nearly every owner I know has a number they watch. It could be the number of calls or customers you get a day, daily billable hours, inventory turns, daily sales, month-to-date production, or individual job costing. Different departments within a business have a critical number as well. Determine your critical number, and then figure out how to track and communicate it.

Employees have to understand this information within the context of the business. For example, in a construction company, taking the first quarter numbers out of context could be horrifying — Bankruptcy for sure. But by midsummer everything should look rosy. The same is true with a retail business dependent upon a good Christmas season.

By training your employees they will understand the "why." There are many ways to get from here to there. For example, *The Great Game of Business* has a workbook called the *YoYo Company* that is particularly good for a manufacturing company. It teaches the basics via the creation of a small business. Some companies send key personnel to seminars to learn how to teach financial information, or they bring in consultants to assist with a training. Other companies have developed skits and board games.

In a company I consulted for, we started a training with the employee's personal P&L's and balance sheets. We taught people about their own income. They learned about variable and overhead expenses, and how to build their equity. By using fictitious people of similar means and profession, we even showed them how to analyze their cash flow budget.

Once the employees learned the basics of their own finances, we moved to the company financial reports. We began to make the connections between employee job performance and how that impacted the numbers. We developed a game which targeted reducing material costs as a percentage of the overall cost-of-goods sold. We started posting the monthly numbers (the score) and then zeroed in on the line item we had targeted, in this case, materials. We posted this line item separately, because this was our critical number, both for the profitability of the business and for the game. The employees could easily see how their performance effected their stake in the game.

Even if there is not full understanding immediately, get your numbers out there. Remember how long it took you to fully understand this stuff? Your employees need to keep seeing the information and working with it. The training has to go beyond the training sessions into daily reality.

Finding the time to do the training is a challenge. Taking the time is expensive. I suggest an initial meeting or two to introduce the open book management concept. Then incorporate the financial education into your regular staff meetings — 15 to 20 minutes at a time. Reinforce this information daily in the field, in the office, or on the shop floor. Talk about it every chance you get. Review, review, review. Start a session by reviewing the last one before you move on to new information. Use a variety of teaching methods. Fill in the forms; count out the numbers; let different people do different parts of the training. Let an employee present the monthly P&L. Pose "what if" questions. What if we could complete this tile job in two days instead of two and a half? What if we did one more service call a week? Take the training right to be bottom line.

You will find some people hungry for this information. Feed them! However, some of your employees will be indifferent or even hostile.

It may be fear — of showing their ignorance, of lack of trust, or of the recognition that the end product of open book management is much more accountability. Some employees will not be able to handle the change and will quit. Some will sit in your meetings oozing negativity. But some will love it. Give yourself a break and preach to the choir. Remember — reinforce the behaviors you want. At some point the negatives will come around or leave. (This might take a private discussion with them on whether or not they want to continue working at your company.)

Until you distribute your first bonus or share your first quarter profits, you will have skepticism. When they see the financial reward for their efforts, things begin to turn around.

Remember — education and communication concerning the financial condition of your company will never end. It will continue to be a critical agenda item in all your meetings. Once you have the basic information out there, give your employees the opportunity to act on it. Your role becomes that of a coach. If you are lucky, you will see an almost immediate change in people's attitudes. They get excited. They think of how they can do things better. They unleash the good idea they have been mulling over for years. They will figure out what to attack and how to do it. They will watch costs. If they need new equipment, they will participate in figuring out if you can afford it. They will track their closing ratios and watch their margins. And you will see that they reap the benefits.

Many companies already have some form of profit sharing. What is missing in most of these companies is the connection between the shared profits and what employees do to create them. The bonuses just sort of materializes at the end of the year, like Santa Claus with a Christmas stocking. With open book management, the employees not only know where it came from, but that they helped to produce it.

I need to stress again that you must tie this to your budget and planning process. For instance, if this is the year you have to buy new equipment and move your operations, you need to know this and have these expenses in your plan. You need to educate your employees on the importance of the long-term viability of the company and how the investments are needed to ensure that there is employment now and in the future. Be sure they understand how investing in the company can contribute to their own job security.

You may want to start this program when things are going well because of the time it takes to get up to speed. Also, it is easier to sell when there is the potential for bonuses and profit sharing. But the ultimate goal is to share the good *and* the bad years. If it is a bad year with no profits, everyone knows there is nothing to share and why. In the years when things go well, everyone benefits.

In Summary

The philosopher Goethe wrote, "Treat a man as he is and he will remain as he is. Treat a man as he can and should be and he will become as he can and should be." Treat an employee as a hired hand and they will be a hired hand. Treat an employee as a partner and owner and they will become a partner and owner. Pretty simple, huh?

Open book management first and foremost takes leadership, commitment, vision, and time. Do you really want to involve your people? Are you really ready to change? Are you able to be totally honest and open — vulnerable? Will you commit the time and resources to make open book management work? Can you see your company and your people in this light? Are you ready to take the leap?

Remember — open book management does not change the structure of a business, only the attitude. Everyone in the company sees and learns to understand the company's financial information, along with all the other numbers that are critical to tracking the business's performance. Employees know that whatever else they do, part of their job is to move those numbers in the right direction. Create games to move those numbers, and then inspect what you expect. Make it fun. (It's been said that the company that makes money has a boss who's funny.) And finally, everyone in the company has a stake in the company's success. Everyone wins, or loses, together.

"TO DO" List

Open Book Management

1. Read the books; talk to others until you really understand the process.

    A. Do you want to take the leap?

2. Do your planning and budgeting, so you can develop fiscally sound games that will positively impact the bottom line.

3. Educate your employees on how your company is run and how it makes money.

4. Set up the training, and schedule it on a weekly basis.

5. Develop games that effect critical areas in your business. Develop the scoring and the stake.

6. What is driving you crazy? What is keeping you up at night?

    A. Write these things down in your notebook, and decide how you can change them.

7. Introduce the games, post scores, and pay people when the games are "won."

8. Be excited. Be exciting!

9. Be a little crazy. Be a cheerleader and a coach.

10. Be persistent. It will take some time to get rolling, but eventually open book management will create a momentum of its own.

    A. It'll take a year. Be willing to hang in there, or don't start.

11. Form an open book management support group in your local neighborhood.

    A. Support is good, and so are other people's ideas.

12. Attend a Gathering of the Games Conference.

    A. Go get excited with people who — just like you — are willing to take the leap to great business in the 21st Century.

Chapter 8

WHO DO YOU NEED?

The beginning is the most important part of the work.

— Plato

A great company has great people in the right positions. One of the owner's jobs is attracting and keeping these people. It is a company wide process that starts with figuring out who you need, then defining roles in relationship to those needs.

Your People Make It Work

I read somewhere once about the 60-30-10 rule. Of the 100% of the employees in the universe:

30% are great. They will go the extra mile, are dependable, reliable, positive and upbeat.

10% are losers. No matter what you do, they will look for the easy way out; won't show; don't care.

60% are in the middle. They will go one way or the other depending on how you treat them.

You want to attract and keep the 30 percenters. The three chapters on personnel, the previous chapter on open book management, indeed, the tone of this whole book is directed at finding and keeping the 30%. They give you a competitive edge, make your company more productive and profitable, and come up with new and better ways to do things.

Yet, some companies design their policies, procedures, and in fact, the whole structure of the business, to mitigate the problems of the 10% rather than support the efforts of the 30%.

What do I mean? — Dress codes, time clocks, no communication, hammering people when they make mistakes, not sharing responsibility, and generally treating people like children. What does this say about your business? How does it undercut you? The 30% you want chafe under these conditions. They want and need responsibility, and will seek a company that treats them like the thinking adults they are. Meanwhile, you hold the 10% in check by all the rules and restrictions — until they figure a way to bend or break them.

And the 60%? How do they respond? It depends on how you treat them. This could be the scenario. The key project due today isn't finished, and it's five o'clock. The 10% say to the 60%, "What do we care? We get paid whether we finish it or not. These guys never pay us for overtime anyway or even give us a pat on the back for going the extra mile. They sure hammer us though when we mess up. The #@#@ with 'em. Let's go have a brew."

In a company structured to attract and keep the 30%, the employees know how the project was bid, and know why it has to be done today. The company recognizes them for the extra effort by a pat on the back, a bonus, or public praise. When someone suggests leaving the work undone, they will respond with, "No way!" They stay and finish the job.

The 10% who don't like this scenario may go to work for your competition. Who needs them? The 30% will love it, and the 60% will soon act more like the 30 percenters.

How do you know which kind of company you are? Read through your personnel policies. Does this sound like a great place to work? Think about your last meeting. Did you fill the agenda with information and training? Did you give people opportunities to share good ideas? Did you engage in public humiliation of the guys who made that big mistake? Do you praise in private (or not at all) and punish in public? Do your employees have the materials and equipment they need to do a good job, or are they asked to make do or cut corners?

Look at what *you* do to create the things that drive you crazy about your employees. Are people late all the time? Are you on time? Do you yell at people for being late or reward people for being on time? Not getting those time cards filled out right? Did you explain why the information is important, or just tell them to DO IT? Did you spend a whole meeting going over how to fill out the time cards, or did you let the people who were doing them right go early and only kept those in need of training?

You set the tone of your business. Catch your employees doing things right. It is more fun for you, and it is more likely to produce the results you want. It creates a positive workplace where people thrive. I am not saying ignore problems; it is how you deal with them that tells the tale. The easiest thing to do is yell, but it is also the least effective way to get the performance that you want and need.

It takes effort and thought to evaluate why someone is having a problem. It takes more time initially to train, to have clear job descriptions, conduct performance reviews, and communicate the company plan. It might take realizing that you are part of the problem. I had one business owner tell me he used to think his employees were the problem. After taking my class, he realized that he was the problem. He was not providing the leadership, direction, and information that his employees needed to be successful.

If your employees are not taking responsibility, look at the word: "response-ability." Are you giving your employees the ability to respond — with knowledge, training, information, opportunity, coaching, feedback, and a stake in the outcome?

You've seen company pyramids looking like this:

The employees were on the bottom: the peons, the cogs in the machine. This pyramid doesn't work anymore. To be competitive in the 21st century your pyramid should look like this:

Your job is to create an environment where your employees can do the best job they can. It is your job to support their efforts, because doing so will make the company successful and profitable. Always remember: *The owner and managers are overhead.* It is the employee who is creating the product or service that makes the company money.

It is also the employee who knows how to do the best job, where money is being wasted, and how to improve the process. It is your job to create an environment where the employee can and will bring their good ideas forward.

Tom Peters tells the following story about a manufacturing company. In the process of empowering the work force, a man came forward with a great idea that increased the effectiveness and efficiency of the production process. Peters went to talk to him. He asked how long the man had worked there. "Eighteen years," the man responded. Peters then asked him how long he'd had the idea. "Eighteen years." A surprised Peters then asked why he had not come forward with the idea before now. The man replied, "No one asked."

Employees are the gold in your gold mine. I believe employees should not be listed as an expense but as an asset. If treated right, people are a renewable resource. They will rise to the level of your expectations. Part of your job is to make people feel good about themselves. You do this by giving them responsibility, letting them know you care, and guiding them to good decisions. You are the coach of your company team. If your team isn't winning, maybe it's the coaching that is the problem.

Attracting and keeping great employees requires mastery of the basics of personnel management. It takes time. *Trust me;* it is time well spent. Making the investment to find and keep great people is one of the best investments you can make.

Creating Your Organization Chart

Often, when I first go into a business I will see an organization chart that looks like this:

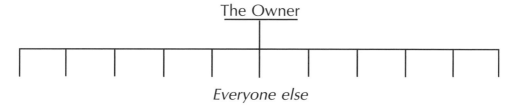

Go back and look at the owner's job description on page 7. If this is your job, how will you have time to do it with this kind of organization? The simple answer is you can't. There are reasons for supervisors and managers. One of them is sanity. Another is profitability.

Profitability? If you are adding expensive supervisors and managers, how can that be? Well, you won't be adding supervisors and managers willy-nilly. What you want to think about is how much money different people cost you. If you earn $50,000 a year, you get paid $26.00 an hour, which is 43 cents a minute. Therefore, anytime you perform work that someone at a lower wage could be doing, you lose money.

Go back to your time analysis (Page 18). What are you doing that someone else could be doing? You need to identify these tasks and push them down the line to your employees. What is your administrative assistant doing that the secretary can do? What is the secretary doing that a receptionist can do? What is your journeyman doing an apprentice can do? What is the apprentice doing that a laborer can do? If you can give some of your responsibilities to your journeyman, and he can do the same to the apprentice, then maybe where you can and need to hire is at the laborer level. The idea here is to maximize the contribution of each person and hire at the lowest, most inexpensive level possible. A laborer making minimum wage makes about a dime per minute. If you pay your journeyman 30 cents a minute and he spends any of his time doing the work of a laborer, you lose money.

Remember the GPM and the triangle (Page 52)? This is one way to improve your GPM without raising your prices. You improve your profitability by having the right wage for the right task. Always hire at the lowest possible wage rate and skill level.

The owner of a small remodeling company told me he could not afford to hire a laborer, because his income was like a roller coaster. He just didn't have time to regularly seek and bid jobs. Instead, he was cleaning up job sites, delivering materials, and gassing trucks! Together, we concluded that hiring someone for a dime a minute and putting himself (at 43 cents a minute) on a consistent timetable to seek and bid jobs, leveled and *improved* his income.

Always look for what you can delegate and to whom. Obviously, this does not mean that you never need to hire at a higher level. In the example above, we might still have to hire an estimator or a supervisor or other management staff. Just look carefully before you automatically hire at the most expensive level. If you have done your planning, where you are trying to go and what you want to accomplish will drive the decision.

You need to remember two other things about your organization chart. First, take into account the span of control: the number of people that one person supervises. There is no set rule for the right number. Just be realistic. It depends on the nature of the work being supervised and the number of responsibilities the supervisor has. It is a balance between sanity and too much overhead.

Second, establish and enforce the chains of command. If you build in a level of management, remember these people now supervise the people below them. You *must* support the actions of the new supervisor. Do not let employees go around the supervisor to you for decisions or undermine what the supervisor had to say. It will not only cause the supervisor to fail, but you will end up with all the work and decisions back on your desk. Support, coach, train, and then let them do their job. Support your chain of command.

Once you have analyzed your employee needs in relationship to your plan and determined your organization chart, you are ready to write your job descriptions.

Creating Your Job Descriptions

Why You Need Them

Job descriptions are a critical part of a successfully run company. Without job descriptions you will have a difficult time answering the following questions. How do you know whom you need, or whom to hire? How can you hold people accountable for getting the job done? How will you know how much to pay people, and when to give them a raise? How can you give people feedback on how well they are doing the job? How can you develop a training program? How will you accomplish your plan? Job descriptions will give you the answers.

How You Write Them

The *process* of developing the job description is just as important as the final product. Jobs do not exist in a vacuum. They relate to and rely on other jobs. Each job has a supplier — someone who provides information or services, and a customer — someone who receives the information and services.

Supplier ⟶ the job ⟶ customer

This is the idea of internal customers and internal customer service.

For example, for a construction job site you would want to develop the laborer, apprentice, and journeyman's job descriptions concurrently, because each job relates to the other. Where does one person's responsibility start and end? Where do people need to work together? Who has primary responsibility and who has backup? These are the kinds of questions and issues you want to address in the development of the job descriptions.

Just as you don't want to develop one job description without considering other jobs in the company, you don't want to write the job description without input from the people involved. Since it is impractical to invite the whole company or division to write the job description, develop the draft with a small team. In the construction example above, the team could include the owner, the superintendent, and perhaps your top journeyman.

Set aside an hour. Put three big sheets of paper on the wall. Write the job title on each sheet. The job description will include the following sections: (See office manager example, pg. 108)

Title: What is the name of this position?

Responsible to: To whom will the person in this position report? This builds in the chain of command. Think in terms of who will participate in the hiring and do the performance review.

Supervises: Who might this person hire, supervise, and evaluate?

Purpose of the position: Why does this position exist? This is a one or two sentence statement. It is often easier to formulate the purpose after you have determined the duties and responsibilities.

Duties and Responsibilities: This is a list of all the things you want this person to accomplish. *Resist the urge to define the job by the person currently in the position.* It is critical that you define the job in terms of the needs of the company; particularly in relationship to the company's goals and plan. If the person currently in the position does not have all the skills or knowledge needed, then the job description helps you identify training needs, the need to move a person, or in some cases the need to terminate. This may sound harsh, but if you do not have the right people where you need them, the overall health and prosperity of the company can suffer; so much so that ultimately, more jobs are in jeopardy.

As your team talks about the jobs, you will be moving back and forth among the three sheets of paper, writing down the various tasks of each job. Use verbs to describe the tasks. For example, do not just list payroll. What does the person do with payroll — deliver the checks, check the timecards, work with the payroll company, or produce the payroll on a weekly basis? Be specific and clear.

Always push the lowest skill level of work to the job that will be the lowest paying. Anytime your highly paid people are doing work a lower skilled and lower paid person can do, you are losing money. If you have done your 15 minute time analysis (which I hope you have), use the analysis as a database for job tasks, and then push work down to the appropriate levels.

You may want to categorize tasks, such as field, administrative, and personnel function. You may also want to create levels within one job description, such as Apprentice 1, 2, and 3, noting increasing levels of responsibility, independence, and skills. This will help later when it comes to salary schedules and making the number of job descriptions manageable.

Be thorough with this list of tasks. Be sure to include not only the skills you require, but behavioral and administrative functions, such as filling out timecards correctly and on time, wearing appropriate clothing, participating in meetings, being courteous to customers, following safety procedures, and so on. Think of the things that drive you crazy with your employees, and you will be able to generate this list very easily. Also, add "Other duties as assigned", because this will never be an all inclusive list.

Results Expected: This is a list of what results you can expect when the employee does the job. Do not use verbs. List the results, not as processes, but as accomplishments. (See example.)

Authority: This section defines how far the employee can go without seeking advice or approval from a supervisor. I have listened to many supervisors complain about employees not having initiative, when in reality the employees would like more responsibility, but they do not feel empowered or directed to take it. This section clears up this confusion. It creates the opportunity to have a great conversation with your employees. As you develop the job description, make sure you give your employees the authority to get the job done. Everyone benefits.

Minimum Qualifications: List here the minimum qualifications a person needs for this job. Be sure to include: certification, licenses, or clean DMV printouts if needed. Only list things you can document or validate such as, number of years experience, time spent supervising, or responsibility for a budget of a certain size. Good people skills may be necessary, but hard to verify on a resume. This section will become part of your hiring procedure. (Page 112)

Date: Always put the date on this and other forms, so that when you make changes (which you will surely do) you will know which is the most current document.

JOB DESCRIPTION
OFFICE MANAGER

TITLE: Office Manager
RESPONSIBLE TO: JAS
SUPERVISES: Receptionist

PURPOSE OF POSITION
To assure the smooth operation of the office and effective use of office staff, materials, equipment and space

DUTIES AND RESPONSIBILITIES
Hires, fires and evaluates receptionist

Arranges for coverage of reception duties as needed

Determines budget for Company office supplies, postage, couriers, maintenance and repairs and monitors expenditures

Responsible for adequacy of office materials and supplies

Responsible for repair and maintenance of office equipment and furniture

Makes recommendations concerning purchase or lease of office equipment and furniture

Plans and supervises office space utilization and moves

Interfaces with property management company

Responsible for management of archival files and storage room maintenance

Other duties as assigned

RESULTS EXPECTED
1. Quality receptionist
2. Adequate materials, equipment and space
3. An effectively run office

AUTHORITY
- 100% authority for receptionist
- 100% for adequacy of materials
- 100% for maintenance of equipment, requires review for lease or purchase
- 100% for use of existing space, requires review for expansion

MINIMUM QUALIFICATIONS

1. Two years office management experience
2. Computer literate

DATE _____

Now type up the information using your word processor. Label it **"DRAFT"**, save it, print it, and then circulate it to your employees. These include the *"suppliers"* and the *"customers."* Ask them for their ideas, additions, questions, and comments. The more they participate in the process, the better the buy-in. When you get their comments back, look them over and incorporate the changes as appropriate. Send the new draft out for one last employee review. Then type up the final product.

Once the job description is written, each supervisor needs to sit down individually with whomever they supervise. Together, they review the employee's job description, being sure to spend plenty of time on results and authority. Answer any questions. Let them know the job description will be the basis of their performance reviews. Then have them sign and date the job description. Give them a copy and put the original in their personnel file.

And never again listen to, "I didn't know that was my job!"

Finally, let everyone read all of your company's job descriptions, including your own. It gives people an appreciation for the role each person plays in a business and how important it is that everyone works together.

"TO DO" List

Getting To the People You Need

1. Review your personnel practices and policies to see whom you are attracting — the 30% or the 10%.

- Make any needed changes.

2. What are you doing to cause or reinforce the employee problems in your company?

- Make a list in your notebook, and vow to act differently in the future.

3. Draw your current organization chart. Now draw one that will help you accomplish your plan and contribute to your profitability; allow you to do your job and maintain your sanity.

4. Write your job descriptions, or review and revise as needed the ones you already have.

5. Review your job descriptions with your employees. Get them signed and into your personnel files.

6. Share job descriptions company wide.

Chapter 9

FINDING THE RIGHT PEOPLE

It's a funny thing about life. If you refuse to accept
anything but the best, you very often get it.

— W. Somerset Maugham

Finding the employee you need is a combination of knowing who you need, defining the position with a job description, and then conducting an effective hiring process. This chapter describes a knock-your-socks-off hiring procedure and information on how to do great interviews.

Your Hiring Practices

Hiring is one of the most important things you do as a business owner or manager. This is true because it is your employees who represent you and your product or service to the customer. It is your employees who determine if you will make a profit or not. It is your employees who decide to do it right or to cut corners. It is your employees who can make your job and life easy or miserable. Unfortunately, people often hire on the spur of the moment, in a panic. The only criterion many employers have for hiring is lack of drool.

Depending on the level of the position, employee turnover can cost a company anywhere from $3000 to $10,000 and more. This includes the time you and your staff will spend in the hiring and interviewing process, the cost of having other people cover a position until you hire someone, and the time it takes to get the new employee up to speed. So, lower your turnover rate by hiring the best person for the job the first time. This takes time, energy, and the commitment to **not** hire the **first** person who walks through the door in your time of need.

In the interim, it may mean that you have to work long hours or incur overtime to get a job done. It may mean that something else on your "to do" list will have to wait a week or two. Whatever it takes to create the time to hire effectively the first time, do it. I will say it again — hiring is the most important thing you do. Do it right, so you don't have to do it over.

What are the consequences of not taking the time to hire right the first time? How about getting the wrong person, spending months in training, getting them up to speed, and then having them quit? What about having an unclear job description, so that the new hire ends up doing what they like to do and not what you need? What about hiring a professional workers' comp claimant like I did? My business ended up with high workers' comp rates and in court fighting a bogus stress claim.

Good hiring starts with a good job description. When employee turnover occurs, it is a great time to evaluate your job descriptions to see if they still reflect the needs of the company. If they don't, add to or modify them as needed, because you cannot hire effectively without a good job description. With a clear job description an applicant knows if they should apply, and you have a good starting point for screening the applicants as well. You also use the job description to help you formulate questions for the interviews. In short, it clearly shows who you need.

Your Hiring Procedure

The following hiring procedure might take a few more days from start to finish, but it will save you time in the long run. It is designed to attract the 30 percenters. Here is how it works, step by step.

1. Placing the advertisement:

First, a hint — Make a list of your advertising sources and keep it in a "hiring procedure" binder. Include the source, phone number, and cost. As you advertise, put a copy of the ad in the binder. You will have a ready source of ads and won't have to recreate the wheel each time.

Your list of advertisers can include local, regional and/or large city newspapers, industry newspapers and newsletters, or the Employment Development Department. Retraining programs, such as the Private Industry Council (PIC), are also useful. If you use PIC they will help you recruit, screen, and train the employee. This is free to the employer. If you want to do the training, PIC will reimburse you for part of the costs, and you may even get a tax credit for hiring an eligible applicant. Other sources are local adult education or community college placement services.

I encourage you to advertise within your company, even if you do not think you have a qualified candidate. It will reinforce your philosophy of employee growth, help you identify who wants to advance, and give you the opportunity to give feedback to employees on how they need to grow in order to advance.

To fill some of your positions, you may also want to consider using an agency that provides temporary employees. This allows you to try out a person before offering regular employment.

Don't forget word of mouth as well: family, friends, colleagues, and, most importantly, current employees. Consider a bonus for an employee who refers a successful candidate to you. The reward could be $100. Half is given when the new employee has made it to three months and the other half at their six-month anniversary. The goal is to have as broad an applicant pool as possible from which to choose.

2. The Ad will read as follows:

Be as descriptive as possible in the ad. Spending a little more money on length will save you time later. Refer to the minimum qualifications you listed in the job description to help make up the ad. For example, the ad for the sample job description on page 108 would read as follows:

> Office Manager needed for busy homebuilder. Two years office management experience and computer literacy required. For application materials, call _____.

3. The application materials consist of the job description, a standard application form, and a cover letter.

Mail, fax, or hand this information to applicants when they inquire about the job. Here's a sample cover letter.

Chapter 9

Dear Applicant,

Thank you for your interest in the position of _____. Enclosed is a description of this position. To apply, please:

1.Read the job description and fill out the enclosed application.

2.Handwrite a one page description of work you have done that evidences your ability to perform this job. Include the name and phone number of a reference.

3.Please include: (any other information you might need, such as copies of licenses, DMV printouts, certifications.)

4.Send the application, the work description, and a resumé to: (your address and/or fax number)

We must receive the above information no later than (date)

> *Sincerely,*

Sending out an application packet accomplishes several things.

A. *It cuts down the amount of time you or your staff spends finding qualified candidates.* When an applicant calls, you do not need to have an extended conversation — A real time waster! Tell them everything they need to know is in the application materials.

Have the application materials already placed in envelopes. When the applicant calls, just write their name and address directly on the envelope and mail it. If you are a small operation with no secretary or receptionist, program your answering machine to say, "If you are calling about the job of _____, please leave your name and address and we will send you the application materials." Then when you have time, pull the names off the machine and mail out the letters.

B. *The procedure screens out unqualified applicants.* If you get 30 phone calls, you will probably get back 15 application packets. This means that there are 15 fewer people to talk to or resumés to review. The job seekers screen themselves out of the running when they read the job description and see the minimum qualifications. Of the 15 applications you get back, one third did not follow the instructions — no handwritten description, no resumé, no certifications, etc. This eliminates the candidate in my book. If they cannot follow these simple instructions, how will they manage to handle the job? From 30 phone calls you are now down to ten application packets to consider seriously.

C. *The procedure attracts the 30 percenters and eliminates the ten percenters.* The 30% see a well-organized company that knows what it wants. You are setting a professional tone, and the good employee wants this job from the get-go. The 10% want to go the other way, because they see an organized company with clear performance objectives and a company that expects results.

D. *The handwritten description of work the applicant has done will help you evaluate the applicant's ability to do the job, and often gives you more information about the person than a professionally typed resumé.* It shows you handwriting, spelling, punctuation, and sentence structure. It also gives you enough information so that you can do some reference checking *before* you do your interviews.

4. As applications arrive, review them briefly.

Get an accordion file with four sections. Label them: "In", "Yes", "No", and "Maybe." Based on a brief review, place the applications in the appropriate section. Before I started doing this, I would have piles of resumés everywhere, and I could never remember which ones I had reviewed. As you place applications in the "No" file, send regret letters right away.

5. Paper screen the applications.

Once you're past your closing date, sit down and go through your "Yes" and "Maybe" applications more thoroughly. First check to see if they meet the minimum qualifications for the job. If the job requires certification or licenses, check to see if the applicant really has them by calling the appropriate licensing or certification board. I had a CPA client who did not check to confirm a CPA license, only to find later that the employee was a professional con artist who had also been "an attorney" and in jail! — Very embarrassing for the firm. If you require a college degree, call the college to verify the degree. If you are hiring a newly graduated high school student, ask them for a transcript. This not only includes courses and grades, but usually an attendance record. This also supports our schools' efforts to hold kids accountable.

As you review the resumé and application, look for time gaps and vague dates or descriptions. Look for illogical career progressions. Look for patterns, such as frequent job changes, short tenures, or lack of specifics.

6. Check references before scheduling interviews.

How often have you interviewed a person who seemed to be the perfect candidate, only to find out later that they steal, have a drinking problem, or an attitude that would try a saint. An in-depth reference check can shine the light of day on these concealed issues. Remember, you can ask a reference nearly anything. The person who is giving the reference is the one who needs to watch what they say. Be sure to ask about performance, attendance, punctuality, getting along with co-workers, and other job related information.

Using the applicant's handwritten description, frame your questions so that the reference can, at least initially, say yes or no. Rather than asking, "What did Jane do in her job?" Say, "In her application Jane wrote that she managed all your bookkeeping and collections. Did she? Did she keep your accounts receivable up-to-date? Overall, did she do well?" It is often hard to get people to give you complete sentences, but they will usually respond to yes and no questions; and generally, as they answer your questions, they loosen up and reveal more.

Also, ask for names of people associated with this person who are not the employer, and therefore not in a position to get in trouble for being candid. For a bookkeeper these might include vendors, a payroll service, or the accountant. If the applicant is a field superintendent on a construction job, it could include subcontractors, building inspectors, people they have supervised, architects, or engineers. Jot down your basic questions prior to making the call and keep notes. You want to be able to remember who said what about whom. Be thorough! Reference checking is a *very* important part of the hiring process.

116

7. Schedule interviews.

Remember, if you received 30 calls and sent out 30 application packets, you probably got 15 packets back. Of these, three to five did not follow instructions, so they went in the "No" file. Of the remaining ten to 12, some did not meet your minimum qualifications, and others did not pass the initial reference check. The final three to five candidates should be worth your time to interview.

You Can Do Great Interviews

Schedule interviews at hour intervals and plan to spend 45 minutes with each candidate. I prefer to interview with another person, so I have someone with whom I can check my perceptions. Some sources say not to do this, because it may make the candidate nervous. But, if the candidate cannot get through a mildly stressful interview, how will they get through a typical day in most businesses? So, it is okay with me if the interview causes some stress.

Set a time and a place where you will not be interrupted. You have spent a lot of time and energy finding these potential employees, so hang in there, and take the time to do the interviews right. Take notes on what people have to say, so you can better remember who said what after the interviews are completed.

Remember, you are the one offering the job. While you want to give the candidate a feel for the job and the company, you do not need to sell them on the job. *They* need to sell *you* on their ability to perform. Give them the opportunity to do so. You need to talk only about 20% of the time. Your job is to listen and learn, not lecture.

Write down all your interview questions before the interview. That way, you will cover everything you want to ask, and you will be consistent with each applicant. If interviewing with another person, decide who will ask what.

Use open-ended questions, ones that start with what, why, or how. Unlike the reference check, avoid asking questions that elicit just a "yes" or "no" response. Follow up on answers, and probe for details. It is also okay for you to be silent. It gets people to offer more information.

Divide the interview into two parts. The first half covers the skills, knowledge, and technical side of the job. In the second half you want to determine if the person will fit into the company culture and be compatible with coworkers.

To come up with the technical questions, go back to the job description. Ask questions that will give you information on the skills, abilities, and the experience needed to do each task. For example, if the job requires the employee to hire, supervise, and evaluate another employee, ask them to describe a situation where they have participated in hiring. Ask how they would deal with an employee discipline problem, or what criteria might they use to determine if a raise is due. If the job includes being able to read blueprints, have a blueprint handy and ask specific questions about the plan. If the job is to effectively install a heater, ask about past experience, types of heaters they have worked on, etc. If the job is to bake bread, ask how many different ways it can go wrong. If it is a sales position, probe into sales techniques and customer service experience.

Also ask questions that relate to educational requirements: Have they taken courses, attended seminars, read the right books, or received awards? Ask about on-the-job achievements and what tasks and job responsibilities they enjoy or dislike. Ask what were the best and worst aspects of their last job? Ask why they left their last job, and what opportunities and work environment are they now seeking. Do they have any concerns about the job for which they are now interviewing or their ability to do it?

At this point, unless you are prepared to train, if the person does not have the technical abilities, knowledge, or skills you need, end the interview. Do not waste your time or theirs conducting the rest of the interview.

If you're satisfied, go on to the second half of the interview, which is designed to determine what kind of person the applicant is. Will they fit into your work environment and company culture? Will they get along well with you and their coworkers? Here are some sample questions:

1. *Why are you interested in us?*

2. *Tell me about your strengths and weaknesses.*

118

3. *Tell me something about yourself. How do you spend a typical day?*

4. *Do you feel that you have made a success of your life? Why?*

5. *What things disturb you most?*

6. *What is the most useful criticism you have ever received? What did you do about it?*

7. *How do you get along with people you dislike?*

8. *What do you like and dislike about your current supervisor?*

9. *What motivates you to make your best effort?*

10. *What is the biggest risk you have taken in recent years?*

11. *What are your plans and dreams for the future?*

12. *Here's a situation that might happen here. How would you handle it?*

Let me give you a few examples. An important characteristic for an employee at my nonprofit for disabled adults was a willingness to give. I asked an applicant why she was interested in us. She told me all the things she expected to get. No matter how I turned the question around, I could not get her to tell me what she had or wanted to give to the agency. Although I had no other candidate, I would not hire her. I had to start the whole hiring procedure again.

In another case, I asked a man what disturbed him most. He told me it was when his wife left the dresser drawers open. A pretty safe answer, except the administrative space we had was about the size of a postage stamp, and no matter how neat and organized we tried to keep it, it was always a little crazy and chaotic. There was no way he would have survived if he couldn't handle those dresser drawers. I didn't hire him.

There are a few things that you **cannot** ask an applicant. Some of these include: age, credit references, birthplace, citizenship (okay to ask if they can legally work), garnishment records, type of military discharge, marital status, childcare problems, plans to have children, housing status (Rent or own?), and physical conditions (i.e., Do you have a physical disability? Have you ever been injured on the job?). People can volunteer this information in the process of answering other questions, but you cannot specifically ask for this

119

information. Believe it or not, people do bring discrimination claims against potential employers for asking illegal questions during the hiring process. So, avoid asking these discriminatory questions.

After interviewing, you may want other people in your organization to meet your top candidates. In my nonprofit corporation I always had the prospective employee spend some time with my staff and disabled clients. You may want them to demonstrate their skills by taking a test — in accounting, computer use, typing, or other job-related tasks.

Once you decide on a candidate, make the job offer. If you have a strong second candidate, don't tell them they don't have the job until the first choice accepts. That way, you'll have a backup if your first choice declines. Also, and this is important, if none of the candidates meet your needs, do not settle for a less than qualified candidate. *Start the whole hiring process again.* As anxious as you may be to fill the position, always remember: hiring is the most important thing you do. Do it right.

Send letters to all applicants, thanking them for their time and interest. Keep the good applications on file for future reference. Then pat yourself on the back for doing a great job hiring a qualified person for the job.

"TO DO" List

What It Takes To Find Great Employees

1. Take the time to hire well.

2. Use the hiring procedure described in this chapter.

3. Check references thoroughly.

4. Prepare for and conduct comprehensive interviews.

5. Find and hire the best. If no "best" appears, start over from the beginning, because hiring is the most important thing you do.

Chapter 10

KEEPING THE BEST OF THE BUNCH

Your job as an owner and manager is not to solve every problem.
Your job is to create a company with compelling problems that
attract bright and unusual people to join in solving them.

— Paul Hawken

You have written the job description, you have done a bang-up job with your hiring and interviewing, and you have found the perfect employee. Through the whole process you have demonstrated to this new employee what a great company you have, what your expectations are, and how well organized you are. We want this reality to flow right into everything else you do. Now that you have a "30 percenter," you want to keep them. This chapter will show you how — from new employee orientation, to wages, to performance reviews, to training.

Your New Employee Orientation

What an employee needs to learn in an orientation will be different for every company. In general, you will probably want to cover at least the following:

1. Go over the company mission statement and annual plan with the new hire. You have recruited and tried to hire a 30 percenter. These people want to know the big picture and where they fit in it. Your mission statement will let them know how to operate on behalf of the company. I am reminded of a commercial builder who believed in working with his subcontractors as partners. He hired a superinten-

dent who had worked for a builder who had a very adversarial relationship with his subs. If the owner had not shared his mission and philosophy with the superintendent, the superintendent might have treated the subcontractors as adversaries instead of as partners. The new employee would not have been successful, not because of a lack of skill but because of a lack of knowledge of how to operate within the business.

2. Have the new hire review their job description and have them sign and date it. Share all the job descriptions in the company and review the organization chart. Explain the salary schedule and when, how, and why you give raises. Discuss performance reviews and when they will occur.

3. Go over all compensation, benefits and personnel policies. Fill out all the forms.

4. Explain the company safety program.

5. Give a tour of all facilities and job sites, and make introductions to key employees and coworkers.

6. If you operate with open book management, explain the philosophy and set up the training schedule.

7. Explain company policies and procedures.

If all this sounds like a lot of time and work, you are right — but only if you think you have to do it all. You don't. Instead, do the following. Make up an orientation checklist. Look at each item on the list and determine the best person to do it. You? Your bookkeeper? The supervisor? A coworker? Then make the new employee responsible for completing the orientation within a specified period of time — a month should do.

Here's how it works. The supervisor goes over the list with the employee. The list includes a column of all the orientation items, a column of who will cover each item, and a sign-off column. (See the example on Page 123.) With the new employee taking the responsibility, the appropriate person signs off each item once it is completed. At the end of the month the supervisor goes over the list once more to be sure it's complete. (The supervisor has penciled this date forward in their "brain".)

New Employee Orientation Checklist

What	Who	Sign-off
Review mission statement	_____	_____
Review company plan	_____	_____
Review and sign job description	_____	_____
Review organization chart and other job descriptions	_____	_____
Review salary schedule and performance review	_____	_____
Review personnel policies and benefit plans	_____	_____
Review safety program	_____	_____
Tour facility	_____	_____
Employee introductions		
co-workers	_____	_____
management staff	_____	_____
Review open book management	_____	_____
Review company policies	_____	_____
Other	_____	_____

What are the advantages of making the employee responsible? Several:

√ It shares the "burden" of conducting a comprehensive orientation procedure.

√ It gives the new employee an opportunity to meet people and become familiar with everyone's roles.

√ It gives the supervisor an early look at the employee's organization and follow-through skills.

√ More important, it gives the employee a very clear message about the kind of company for which they work. They work for a company where they are expected to take responsibility; one where they are expected to know their job and how it fits in with and supports everyone else's. They know where the company is heading and what they need to contribute to its success. They know everything a 30 percenter needs to know. If you accidentally hired a ten percenter, they know it is time to get out!

In a company where everyone is pulling toward success, you must be consistent in all aspects of the business — from the mission to the job description, to hiring, to orientation process.

How to Pay Your Employees

Most business owners I have worked with don't want to think about wages. Their policy on raises is based on who complained the loudest and most recently. But, how you pay your people is critical. It drives the kind of employee you attract and keep. Your wages are also major line items on your P&L. If the wages are direct costs, increases affect your GPM. Overall, they affect how much you need to sell to break even. By not having a clear policy on wages and raises, you spend too much time and energy agonizing over who to pay what, and it makes it harder to anticipate the numbers on you P&L.

Wage Schedules

Establish wage schedules based on the level of contribution an employee makes. Don't let an employee's longevity status sway you away from this idea. (Note: treat salary schedules in the same manner.)

Let me explain. A construction site has laborers, apprentices, and journeymen. Each job is critical to the completion of the project. But a journeyman brings more education, skills, and abilities to the job than the laborer. They contribute more to the company's competitive edge. Consequently, a journeyman's wages will be higher than the laborer. Thus, wage determination begins with a job description.

Look at your job descriptions in terms of skills and experience. Then look at the job's contribution to the success, profitability, and value of the company. Then, keeping prevailing wages in your area in mind, give a salary range to each job. Let's say that in your area a laborer earns from $6.00 to $8.00, the apprentice $8.00 to $12.00, the journeyman $12.00 to $20.00. When you start an untrained person as a laborer, you start them at $6.00. When they can do everything on the job description without supervision they will be at the top — $8.00. You cannot pay more than $8.00 for a person contributing to your company as a laborer, because it will make you less competitive in the marketplace. Remember the GPM/ sales/ overhead triangle? High direct costs/wages will reduce the GPM. High overhead costs/wages affect the break-even sales you need. Thus, your salaries and hiring decisions are tied to your financial and budget considerations, which connect to your plan.

The point is that you cannot afford to pay a laborer the same wage as a journeyman even if the laborer has been with you for 20 years. The only way the laborer can make more than $8.00 an hour is if there is an overall increase in the company salary schedule based on cost-of-living adjustments, or the person decides to acquire more skills — by, for example, becoming an apprentice. In the above example the wage range for an apprentice is $8.00 to $12.00. When the employee can do the apprentice job competently, they will reach the $12.00 wage. Until they begin to learn the skills required of a journeyman, they cannot earn over $12.00 an hour. What they earn has to be based on the value of their contribution to the productivity and profitability of the company.

Communicate to your employees how your pay schedule is tied to the job description. Explain that how much they are able to earn is dependent upon company success and profitability and the skills they bring to the table. If they want to earn more they need to develop their skills. Then when a higher paying job opens up, they could apply and perhaps be promoted.

By being clear about how much money people make and how they can earn more, the responsibility for increases in wages belongs to the employee. It is no longer the "squeaky wheel that gets the grease."

Salaried Versus Hourly Wages

Some employers confuse wages with salary. They think that by paying an employee by the month instead of hourly that the employee is a salaried worker who is exempt from overtime rules. **This is not the case.** You must compensate workers for overtime based on specific criteria from the U.S. Department of Labor and individual state labor departments. Overtime claims are very common, so it is very important to be sure that employees who are not paid overtime are truly exempt from legal overtime requirements.

As of this writing, there are four types of jobs exempt from overtime: executive, administrative, professional, and outside sales.

The following is a brief summary of some of the criteria for the exempt positions. You should consult an employment law attorney for more specific information about this complex issue. You will begin to see another reason why your job descriptions are so important.

In an executive position — owner, manager, superintendent — the primary duty must be to manage an enterprise or department. The person must direct at least two other workers and has the authority to hire and fire, or their recommendations must carry significant weight. The person must also have and use discretionary powers.

Exempt administrative positions must directly relate to management or general business operations, use discretion and judgment in the performance of "intellectual work", and directly assist the owner, or an executive or administrative employee. "Intellectual work" in this context means office or nonmanual work directly related to management policies or general business operations. This could be an administrative assistant like an office manager who has the power to make decisions on important matters independent of an immediate supervisor.

In the professional category, employees are required to have advanced knowledge acquired by specialized study. The work is original and creative, and results depend on invention, imagination, or talent. Once again, the work requires discretion and judgment, is intellectual, varied, and results are not standardized. Accountants, engineers, and architects, belong here.

The final exempt category is outside sales. To qualify for this category, the employee must be away from the employer's place of business making the sales or getting the orders for a certain percentage of their time.

In each category the exempt work *must be a certain percentage of what the person does.* This varies from state to state and for federal law. Federal law requires the exempt work to comprise at least 80% of what the person does. Otherwise, the position becomes eligible for overtime pay.

Compliance with labor laws and standards is complicated. I am not even going to get into travel time, independent contractors, the American with Disabilities Act, piecework, or sexual harassment. This book is not a legal manual for personnel related law. The laws change too frequently. *What you need to know is that lack of knowledge is not an argument or excuse for lack of compliance.* And being out of compliance can cost you big bucks, and overtime is a favorite issue. So, check with a good, employment-law attorney about specific concerns or problems.

Other Ways to Compensate Your Employees and Why

I'm sure it comes as no surprise to you that surveys from a variety of industries show time and again that money is not the number one thing people want from their jobs. What comes first is appreciation of their work, feeling "in on things", job security, and meaningful work. You can compensate people in these areas by sharing the annual plan, writing clear job descriptions, delegating responsibilities, communicating information, or implementing open book management. Benefits, incentives, and performance reviews are direct and unmistakable rewards.

Benefits

Benefits are crucial to employees. Besides the required benefits of social security, disability, and workers' compensation, most businesses provide some form of health benefits, vacation and/or sick leave, and paid holidays. Employers can score a lot of points by promoting benefit programs and communicating the costs to provide these benefits to their employees.

Unfortunately, my confidential interviews with employees often reveal a lack of clarity about what benefits are provided, and a lack of knowledge on the costs of these benefits to the company. Since we know recruitment and turnover are very expensive, and good, long-term employees are a huge asset, educating them about their benefits is time well spent. This is a real opportunity for some *internal marketing*. Owners should not only tell their customers how wonderful the business is, they should also tell their employees. You can do this periodically by reviewing the benefits at your weekly meetings. Remember to also let people know how much these benefits cost. (See Chapter 7.)

Incentives and bonus programs

Although I covered this topic in detail in the Open Book Management Chapter, I want to say here that bonuses or incentives can reward employees and not result in a permanent expense item in your budget. In contrast, a raise obligates the employer to an ongoing expense. Tying bonuses to company performance and profitability is an excellent long-term strategy that benefits both the employee and the company.

Incentives and rewards do not always have to cost money. Some non-financial rewards include:
- √ **Genuine and frequent "Thank You's"**
- √ **More opportunities for input**
- √ **Flexible hours**
- √ **Better tools or equipment**
- √ **A Meaningful training of their choice**
- √ **Business travel**
- √ **Letters of commendation**
- √ **Public recognition of a job well done**
- √ **Afternoon or day off of their choosing**
- √ **Remembering anniversaries or birthdays**
- √ **Flowers, dinners, theater tickets**

Be creative. Tie the acknowledgment to what the employee enjoys. Getting a lawn mower motivated one guy I know, but it sure wouldn't work for me! Knowing your employees is part of being an effective manager. Would they like opera tickets or baseball tickets? Is it dinner for two or a round of golf? Take the time to know your employees. Always remember, they are one of your most important assets.

Doing Your Performance Reviews

Employees want and need feedback on their performance. Yet, I have seen some of the best examples of procrastination when it comes time to do performance reviews. Take heart. Once you learn the skill it's not so bad, and you will get better and better at it.

It helps to have a clearly written job description which you have reviewed with your employee, because you can turn the job description into the performance review by the magic of cutting and pasting. Since the job description states what you want the employee to do, by turning it into a performance review you have a clear guide for evaluating the employees performance. The next section shows how the do the cut and paste.

Creating Your Own Evaluation Tools

First, bring up the job description on your word processor. (See the job description example on page 108 and the performance review example on page 132.) Then:

1. On the top, change *Job Description* to *Performance Review*

2. Add in *Employee name and Date*. Leave *Title*

3. Delete *Reports to* and replace with *Evaluated by*

4. Leave in *Objective* and *Duties and Responsibilities*

5. Under each duty and responsibility paste in the following:

Excellent ❑ Good ❑ Satisfactory ❑ Needs Improvement ❑

Comments: _____

_____

You are creating an evaluation tool based on what you've already told the employee the job is. This will make the performance review easier, because unlike a generic evaluation format, the performance review format I'm showing you here is tailored from each job description.

6. Paste "excellent, good, etc." in the *Authority* section as well. Delete the *Minimum qualifications and Results Expected* sections.

7. An employee needs, not only good skills, but appropriate behaviors. They may be great, fast, and accurate, but if they are always late, make customers angry, or do not get along with other employees, you need to tell them. So, let's add a section to the performance review that addresses these attributes. Paste in the following:

Work quality and quantity:

❑Excellent ❑ Good ❑ Satisfactory ❑ Needs Improvement

Comments: _____

_____

Dependability:

❑Excellent ❑ Good ❑ Satisfactory ❑ Needs Improvement

Comments: _____

_____

Initiative and flexibility:

❑Excellent ❑ Good ❑ Satisfactory ❑ Needs Improvement

Comments: _____

_____

Skills and job knowledge:

❑Excellent ❑ Good ❑ Satisfactory ❑ Needs Improvement

Comments: _____

_____

Personal relationships:

❑Excellent   ❑ Good   ❑ Satisfactory   ❑ Needs Improvement

Comments: _____

_____

Attendance and punctuality:

❑Excellent   ❑ Good   ❑ Satisfactory   ❑ Needs Improvement

Comments: _____

_____

Supervisory skills:

❑Excellent   ❑ Good   ❑ Satisfactory   ❑ Needs Improvement

Comments: _____

_____

8. Finally, you need a place to summarize what needs to happen next for both the employee and yourself. So paste in the following:

Additional comments/improvement plan as needed. Include several lines for writing the improvement plan.

9. Finally, you need to have the employee acknowledge that the review was conducted. So add:

I have reviewed this evaluation

_____   _____

Employee signature   Date

_____   _____

Evaluator signature   Date

See how easy that was? Now all you have to do is make the appointment with your employee and do the review.

Performance Review
Office Administrator

Employee Name_____ Date_____

Title: **Office Administrator**

Evaluated by _____

Objective

To assure the smooth operation of the office and effective use of office staff, materials, equipment, and space

Duties And Responsibilities

Hires, fires and evaluates receptionist

❑Excellent ❑ Good ❑ Satisfactory ❑ Needs Improvement

Comments: _____

_____

Arranges for coverage of reception duties as needed

❑Excellent ❑ Good ❑ Satisfactory ❑ Needs Improvement

Comments: _____

_____

Determines budget for company office supplies, postage, couriers, maintenance and repairs, and monitors expenditures

❑Excellent ❑ Good ❑ Satisfactory ❑ Needs Improvement

Comments: _____

_____

Responsible for adequacy of office materials and supplies

❑Excellent ❑ Good ❑ Satisfactory ❑ Needs Improvement

Comments: _____

Responsible for repair and maintenance of office equipment and furniture

❑Excellent ❑ Good ❑ Satisfactory ❑ Needs Improvement

Comments: _____

_____

Makes recommendations concerning purchase or lease of office equipment and furniture

❑Excellent ❑ Good ❑ Satisfactory ❑ Needs Improvement

Comments: _____

_____

Plan and supervises office space utilization and moves

❑Excellent ❑ Good ❑ Satisfactory ❑ Needs Improvement

Comments: _____

_____

Interfaces with property management company

❑Excellent ❑ Good ❑ Satisfactory ❑ Needs Improvement

Comments: _____

_____

Responsible for management of archival files and storage room maintenance

❑Excellent ❑ Good ❑ Satisfactory ❑ Needs Improvement

Comments: _____

_____

Other duties as assigned

❑Excellent ❑ Good ❑ Satisfactory ❑ Needs Improvement

Comments: _____

Work quality and quantity

❑Excellent   ❑ Good   ❑ Satisfactory   ❑ Needs Improvement

Comments: _____

_____

Dependability

❑Excellent   ❑ Good   ❑ Satisfactory   ❑ Needs Improvement

Comments: _____

_____

Initiative and flexibility

❑Excellent   ❑ Good   ❑ Satisfactory   ❑ Needs Improvement

Comments: _____

_____

Skills and job knowledge

❑Excellent   ❑ Good   ❑ Satisfactory   ❑ Needs Improvement

Comments: _____

_____

Personal relationships

❑Excellent   ❑ Good   ❑ Satisfactory   ❑ Needs Improvement

Comments: _____

_____

Attendance and punctuality

❑Excellent   ❑ Good   ❑ Satisfactory   ❑ Needs Improvement

Comments: _____

_____

_____

Supervisory skills

❑Excellent   ❑ Good   ❑ Satisfactory   ❑ Needs Improvement

Comments: _____

_____

Additional comments/improvement plan as needed

❑Excellent   ❑ Good   ❑ Satisfactory   ❑ Needs Improvement

Comments: _____

_____

_____

I have reviewed this evaluation:

_____

Employee signature   Date

_____

Evaluator signature   Date

Conducting the Performance Review

Timing

Let's say you just hired a new employee named Bridget. I suggest that you do her first review three months after you hire her. This honeymoon period is a great time to ensure that Bridget is on track with her job and your expectations. After this initial review, do the formal reviews annually. You will meet with Bridget sooner if problems arise, or the job changes, or to applaud improvements that came out of the three-month or annual review.

Scheduling reviews every six months may sound like a good idea, but I think you will find it difficult and not really necessary. Be realistic; plan them annually and during your slow season. If Bridget's annual date lands in your busy season because of when you hired her, do a one-time shift to an earlier date to get her into your regular cycle. If you run a gift shop, you don't want to do a review in November, even if you did hire Bridget last Thanksgiving.

Believe me, Bridget knows when her review is coming up. Still, give her a week to several days advance notice anyway. Schedule an uninterrupted hour for the review, even though you may not use the whole time. This is a very important meeting; so don't rush. Relax.

Who does the review

Bridget's supervisor does the review. Let's say that's you. You may seek feedback from other people who work closely with Bridget, particularly if there is a major problem. You may even want to role-play all or part of the review with someone. However, don't pussyfoot; do the review yourself.

Let's hope Bridget's doing a bang-up job. If not, and if the review could result in her termination, you may want someone else present as a witness. I called someone in when I did the review of Oscar, a "professional" workers' compensation claimant I had to terminate. It let him know we were serious, and more important, it kept me from leaping across the desk or indulging in some other equally inappropriate behavior.

How to do the review

First, fill out your new performance review form. Some employers will have the employee fill one out in advance and will use this as part of the process. It may give you insight on where you and the employee are in agreement. Often the employee is harder on themselves than you would be. It can also make your job more difficult if you see big discrepancies between your and your employee's perceptions. You need to decide what works best for you.

Consider each item. Is Bridget doing an excellent, good, or satisfactory job, or does she need improvement? There seems to be real resistance to checking the "excellent" or "needs improvement" spaces. If you have checked "good," ask yourself what she would need to do to be excellent. If you can come up with how she could improve, write it in the comments' section. If you cannot think of any way for her to improve, mark the "excellent" space. That's why it's there. Add a comment as to why this is an area of excellence. The comment line is for good and bad performance. For example, even Bridget's excellent performance could improve if she took on additional responsibility.

You may also hesitate to mark the "needs improvement" space. Remember, marking this space is not saying Bridget is a bad person, only that she needs to improve in this area. You need to be specific about what the problem is. Is it lack of training? Was it something that you never fully delegated or explained? Is Bridget lazy or careless? If you do a good job with this review, you will find that at least some of the reasons Bridget's performance needs improvement are because you have not provided the tools, resources, training, or support for her to be successful. A good review usually results in both the employee and the supervisor adding a few things to their "TO DO" list.

When you come to the "Additional comments, improvement plan" portion of the review, go back and look things over. Here, you are going to summarize and state clearly what your expectations are. Be specific and use dates. Let me give you some examples.

Let's talk about Bridget & Horace

1. Bridget is your bookkeeper and you've made it clear to her that you want certain financial reports at specific times during the month. She

finishes your P&L and aging reports on time, but she has been unsuccessful in getting the cash flow projections to you. You realize you have never really explained what it is you want or where she can get all the needed information. The improvement plan will be for you or your accountant to train Bridget over the next month. After the training, you expect to receive the cash flow report on a weekly basis, beginning the second month after the review.

2. Horace, the service manager is always late to work by ten to twenty minutes. The comments' section would say "We need to see an immediate improvement in being to work on time. Your continued tardiness will result in discipline, up to and including termination." (See section on discipline for more detail: Page 147.) There is no training needed here. It's Horace's problem. Your job is to be very clear that you will no longer tolerate this behavior.

Follow-through is critical. Too often, once the review is done, you file it, only to discover a year later that Horace is still dragging in late, and Bridget still hasn't produced a cash flow projection on time.

Schedule for your follow-ups during the reviews. For example, you would schedule time in your "brain" for Bridget's training during her review. For Horace you would schedule a weekly, five-minute meeting to review his on-time behavior. Require Bridget and Horace to write down these follow-up activities also. This assures each of you that the follow-ups will occur. If an improvement plan requires that an employee gets training or practice with someone other than you, and they are to take responsibility to insure the training occurs, you would write down in your "brain" follow-up check points for these activities as well. Follow-up assures improvement in performance, thus making the review a good use of your time and not just a fruitless exercise.

How and When to Give Your Employees Raises

Contrary to the norm, I do not believe in giving raises when you do the performance review. If you just told Bridget she needs to make an improvement and then immediately give her a raise, where is the incentive to make the improvement? I recommend you consider a raise six months after the performance review. This gives Bridget six months to start churning out those reports. In six months (which you noted in your "brain") you review only the areas in her performance review that needed improvement. If her performance improved, then you can consider a raise. (If there is money available and if it fits in with your salary schedule.) By separating the review and the raise, you also get Bridget's attention twice a year instead of once. You keep her focused on constant, individual improvement.

In reality, I support paying people based on the value they bring to the business. All "raises" should be in the form of bonuses or profit sharing based on the success of the business and meeting company and/or department goals. Review the information on open book management for reminders on how this works.

I believe we owe it to our employees to give them opportunities to grow and learn and improve their skills. Remember, we want to attract and keep the 30 percenters. To do so, performance reviews are an absolute must. Just do it!

Training

Why train? Well, for starters, it attracts and keeps those 30 percenters. It contributes to growth in your people, those wonderful assets within your business. It helps to keep your company competitive, and it's a bargain to boot.

If the thought of providing training overwhelms you, keep in mind that you don't have to do it all. You provide the leadership. You determine it is an important value. You create the line item in your budget. Beyond this, training can be a group effort.

How do you determine your training needs? It's easy. Ask your employees. They have all sorts of good ideas. For example, I was consulting in an electrical company when an employee named Leroy fessed up that he didn't know how to use a machine that bent metal pipe. It turned out the employees weren't using many of the tools the owner thought they were. So the owner incorporated tool training into the weekly meetings. I was there the day we got to bend a bunch of pipe. It was great! We had an employee, who knew how to use the machine, do the training. (More on trainers in a bit.)

If you have created an open environment with the ideas in this book, employees like Leroy will be forthcoming with their training needs. When you ask at your regular meetings or in performance reviews, "What would you like to learn?", you'll get an answer.

Keep in mind that training does not always have to be job specific. A plumber really wants to learn computers? Go for it. The cost to your company for the tuition and books for a community college computer class, when compared to the benefits to the company, is an easy cost/benefit ratio to figure. Who knows, the day your computer is acting funny, the plumber may have the answer. Add to this the growth in confidence, self-esteem, and loyalty to the company, and it becomes an even better investment.

There is so much people want and need to know. Ask your management staff for their ideas. Review your callbacks and other mistakes for clues on training needs. If you are doing open book management, financial training will be on your list. Training can include education on your company plan, or review of company job descriptions. An annual review of company procedures is also time well spent. Don't forget the internal-marketing opportunities, such as reviewing your benefit programs and how to use them.

Be creative. Think "out of the box." For example, think about the personal skills needed for communication, conflict resolution, creativity, or managing change. Training in personal development reaps great benefits for both the individual and the company. Get personal development audiotapes and put them in your company vehicles, and allow them to go home. Set up an in-house library of books and tapes. Create a minibonus for listening to or reading them. Subscribe to a TV station that has only educational and personal development programming. Set it up and write off the above as a business expense. Make a goal of your training to enhance who people *are*, not just what they *know*.

Generate a list of training opportunities, then put them in order of importance. Use the list to create your training program for the year. If appropriate, plan to do the training at your weekly meeting or at special in-house training sessions; or seek outside training to fill the need.

You will be amazed at how much you can do internally. Look at the training and ask, "Who can provide this?" Is "Sarah" your best electrician? Have her do the training on the trick wiring techniques that make her so efficient. One of your salesclerks, "Jim", does creative merchandising? Let him do the training.

Want to provide more information on your benefits program? Have someone from your health plan provider do a presentation. Want to teach loan agents about the newest real-estate loan programs? Have the loan officer from the bank do the training. Want to educate your sales staff on good customer service? Bring in an outside trainer or send your people out to a workshop like mine. Can only send one or two? Then have them do a presentation when they get back on what they learned. Owners and managers seem to attend workshops a lot. Give your front-line and field people this opportunity to grow as well. Take them with you.

Need basic training for your employees? Join your trade or professional association. They may have it or you could be the one to add the extra push they need to begin offering it. What else does your trade or professional association offer? What about your local community college? Have people take classes in the evening. Tell them you will pay for the tuition and books when they bring you their passing grade.

There are people like me who will design a training to meet your specific needs. Want your plumbers to be salespeople? I already taught sales and customer service, so I redesigned a class to meet this particular need for a local plumbing and heating trade association.

Keep in mind, especially as you develop your in-house training, that people learn in different ways; they have a preferred way to process information. It can be auditory — by listening: visually — by seeing: tactile — by touching or handling: or even kinetically — by having to move around and do things. I used to think I was a visual learner because I write things down. I thought I needed to see it. More recently I realized I am a tactile learner. It is the physical act of writing it down that makes me remember, helps me to learn. I am a terrible auditory learner. It goes in one ear and out the other. I have to write things down to learn.

If you do your own trainings, keep in mind that as you talk people will be using their auditory mode of learning, but you must also use charts, overheads, and other written materials, so people can use their visual

141

mode of learning. In addition, have people take notes to take advantage of their tactile mode, and you can let them do hands-on activities, like bending that pipe, so they can use their kinetic mode. By using multiple learning modalities, the trainee is more likely to learn, recall, and use the information; and that is, after all, what we are after.

Remember the tone you are trying to create in your company. The positive, fun, organized, productive, profitable company that attracts and keeps the great 30% of employees. Make an investment in time and money to provide training. It will pay you back beyond your investment and expectations. *Trust* me; this too I know from experience.

When running my nonprofit corporation, there was never enough money for wages. I told my staff that although I could not promise them high wages, I could promise them that they would leave the agency with more skills. I kept my promise. I had great employees, low staff turnover, and a nationally recognized program — all thanks to my employees' efforts. I believe the commitment to staff training contributed greatly to our success. It will with your company as well.

"TO DO" List

What It Takes to Keep Great Employees

1. Create an orientation check list and do great employee orientations.

2. Create a salary schedule for all the jobs in your company and communicate this to all employees.

3. Create your performance review forms.

4. Do annual performance reviews and follow up on needed improvements.

5. Tie raises to improved performance and increased contribution to the company, or eliminate them all together and share the profits.

6. Be sure to communicate your benefits and their costs to your employees. Do your internal marketing.

7. Set up your annual training program.

Chapter 11

KEEPING YOUR COMPANY LEGAL

Success covers a multitude of blunders.

— George Bernard Shaw

Your company does not exist in a vacuum. It exists in a sea of rules, laws, and regulations that are complex and demanding. You must navigate this sea as effectively as possible to survive and thrive. Here are some the things to know to sail safely in these waters.

Your Personnel Policies

Personnel policies, whether contained in employee handbooks, employee agreements, or distributed in memos, describe policies within your company that relate to your employees, your employment practices, your benefit program, and other issues and expectations. It is important to remember that your personnel policies are a part of the contract of employment between you and your employees and therefore have *legal* significance. If you end up with a disgruntled employee who sues you for whatever reason, these policies will be very important in protecting yourself or defending your case. I had an owner tell me once that he didn't want all this stuff in writing because he didn't want to be held to it. The problem with this idea is that everything that comes out of your mouth and the employees interpretation of what you said becomes your official policy. Even with written policies, an employee could make a case that you *said* they had a job for life, and now they want to hold you to it. If you have good personnel policies, you will at least have a fighting chance to prove otherwise.

Personnel policies not only protect your business from a legal standpoint, they also serve as a means for clearly communicating vital information to your employees about what your expectations are for them and what they can expect from you.

The following are common items in personnel policies:

♦ An equal opportunity statement, a policy on harassment, information on the Americans with Disabilities Act (ADA), and other such regulatory language the government comes up with.

♦ An "at will" statement, which is legal language that says that the employee/employer relationship can be terminated at any time with or without cause. (This is more complicated than it seems.)

♦ An arbitration policy. The main advantage of arbitration is that it is a less costly and more speedy method of resolving disputes than the state and federal court systems. Employees do not give up their legal rights. They merely agree to submit them to an arbitrator rather than a judge and jury.

♦ Categories of employment. You need to define full-time, part-time, and seasonal workers. This is important, because this will have an impact on, for example, who is eligible for benefits. I have seen policies without this clarification that implied everyone was eligible for the company health and retirement plan when only covering full-time employees was what the employer had in mind.

♦ A description of wage and hour policies. Include paydays, advances (none!), overtime, and on call.

♦ A description of "away from work" benefits, such as holidays — paid or not vacations — paid or not sick days — paid or not jury duty and medical leave, which includes pregnancy leave.

♦ A description of other benefits: like those required by law, such as workers' comp and disability and those you voluntarily provide, such as medical, dental, profit sharing, and retirement. Be sure to describe who is eligible and when. For example, are full-time employees eligible for health insurance after three or after six months of employment? What share of the cost does the company cover?

♦ Describe your "on the job" expectations, such as a drug and alcohol policy, uniforms, working hours, attendance and punctuality, breaks, personal phone calls, and smoking.

If this sounds like a lot of work, it is. However, there are many ways to get these policies written. Some payroll services offer personalized employee handbooks, and they will update them as the laws change. You can hire a professional personnel company to do them with you. You can hire an employment law attorney to write them for you. There are computer programs with boilerplate policies that you can cut and paste and personalize. You can cut and paste someone else's policies. If you do either of the last two options, I *strongly* recommend that you have an employment law attorney review them before you issue them. Then have your policies reviewed annually to ensure that they are up-to-date with the latest legal language and requirements. Remember, these are legal documents that may be scrutinized in court someday.

Besides being a method to entice a new employee, the benefits you offer are also a great internal marketing tool. For example, you can structure your benefits to promote loyalty and longevity by escalating benefits for long-term employees. If you provide a paid vacation benefit of one week after one year of employment, increase it to two weeks after five years and three weeks after ten years. Sick leave? How about if they don't use it, add some or all of it to their vacation time. Paid health insurance? How about picking up the spouse or family after a period of time. Benefits can be as important as wages for many employees. Expensive? Yes, but remember the value of a well trained and knowledgeable long-term employee.

Establishing personnel policies with an employee handbook pushes you to establish consistent employment practices. Making it up as you go along can cause all sorts of problems, both legal and emotional. Think through your polices without considering any particular employee. Keep in mind instead, what is fair for all and what you can afford. Then, when an employee approaches you with a concern, you can refer to the policy, and not to the emotion of the moment. Your response can be fair, consistently applied from employee to employee, and help keep you out of legal hot water. It would be nice if we didn't need this kind of thing, but it is just not that way anymore. So protect you and your business by getting or reviewing your policies as soon as possible.

Your Personnel Files

It is really amazing how all the stuff about and for your employees accumulates. You need to put all this paper somewhere, because you never know when you will need to find it. Some of it is for your convenience, some for your employee, and some for legal purposes.

Things that go into each person's personnel file include:

♦ The employment application

♦ The W-4

♦ Personal information and whom to contact in emergencies

♦ The orientation checklist

♦ The signed job description

♦ The legal requirements, such as the I-9 employment eligibility verification form, and SB 198 safety forms

♦ Signed performance reviews

♦ Copies of required licenses and certificates

♦ DMV print out if needed

♦ Salary and raise history

♦ Personnel policy receipt and signed "at will" statement

♦ Documentation of disciplinary actions if applicable

♦ Exit interviews if conducted

You need to keep this information under lock and key. You will not only end up with confidential information from reviews and/or disciplinary actions in the file but with other information you don't want to lose. I learned this the hard way. I had an employee out on a workers' comp claim for an ankle problem that I knew from various conversations was a preexisting condition. When I went to get his application to confirm this, I found his application missing from my unlocked files. I had no way to verify what I knew was true. This guy turned out to be a "professional" workers' comp claimant. I was not the first employer to support him. We ended up in court. I would love to have had that application, but I didn't. I did by then, however, have my personnel files in a locked cabinet, but in this case it was locking the gate after the animals escaped.

You should also review your files annually to make sure you have the latest copies of licenses and certificates, and that personnel information is current. Attached to each file, I had a form with years listed across the top and a list of everything I wanted in the file down the side. Annually, I would check to see that each thing on the list was in the file and update things as needed. (A perfect way to spend your time when it is slow or you are procrastinating on another task, but don't want to be totally nonproductive.) Unfortunately, unless you are big enough to have a personnel department or human resources person, this is one task you should not delegate because of the confidential nature of the information in the file. Just pencil the job into your "brain" annually to make sure it gets done.

You should keep your personnel files for four years. At the time of this publication, the law requires that you keep some things for only three years but that makes it complicated. If you want specific details, go see your employment law attorney or personnel expert. I'm into keeping it simple; so four years works for me.

How to Discipline and Terminate an Employee

Most likely, no matter how well you have hired, supervised and evaluated, you will have to deal with employee discipline or a termination. Before you discipline or terminate an employee, there are several things you may want to consider.

First, are you contributing in any way to the problem? There is some interesting literature about the addictive organization in which the roles played out in the workplace are similar to the ones played out in addictive relationships. The one I see most in companies is "enabling" behavior. Enabling behavior is when one person acts to cover up or excuse someone else's actions. For example, in an alcoholic relationship, enabling occurs when one person's actions enable or allow the alcoholic to continue drinking. The enabler may call the boss with excuses on the morning of a hangover, make excuses to the children, or apologize to friends.

Enabling behavior in the workplace may take the form of doing someone's work for them. Picture competent Rosie, the office manager, picking up the slack for Horace, who is lazy or unorganized. Rosie is enabling Horace to goof-off. A supervisor, let's say you, can do this in many ways: excuse Horace, let it slide this time, do Horace's thinking for him, never deal with an issue, or let the past cloud the present. Ultimately, the behavior you have been ignoring or enabling will bring you or good old Rosie to the point of such frustration that all you want to do is fire Horace. Yet for him, the pink slip may come out of the blue.

Other things that may be contributing to the problem were mentioned in the performance review section, but it is worthwhile to recall them here. These include a lack of training, a lack of tools or resources, unclear expectations, or things out of the employee's control, such as too much work or poor internal customer service. If not dealt with in the performance review, these performance problems can escalate to a disciplinary problem.

So consider everything before you move forward with disciplinary action. Also please note: *Depending on the circumstances, it may make sense to get legal advice at any point in the disciplinary process but particularly so prior to an actual termination.* Even if you win, a wrongful discharge claim can be expensive. The more professional you are in this process, the less likely that the employee will consider a wrongful discharge claim. This is a good place to err on the side of caution. Spend some money and get expert legal advice from an employment law attorney.

Given that you have spent so much time in hiring, orienting, and working with an employee, the goal of a disciplinary process may be, if possible, to save the relationship. If this is the goal, use progressive discipline. (I'll explain shortly.) If the problem is too great — such as drinking on the job, jeopardizing someone's safety, drug use, or anything else you have defined in your personnel policies as grounds for immediate dismissal, then do it. You do not have to go through the following steps for all circumstances. However, even with an immediate dismissal, it is still wise to seek legal counsel. It is *critical* to document the reason for the termination and keep it in the employee's file.

If you hope to rehabilitate the relationship, then progressive discipline is an option. Remember, you don't have to go through these steps *unless* the employee handbook specifically states that progressive discipline will be followed in *each* instance of discipline. You might want to *avoid written* progressive discipline policies, as they can be interpreted to contradict an at-will policy of employment. Given that caveat, it can be a useful tool to resolve a problem. It works like this:

1. *Verbal warning.* At all times in the process be very specific about what the problem is, what your expectations are for change, and the potential consequences. In the verbal warning you discuss the problem with the employee and make a note of the conversation in your "brain." For example — "John, I see you are without your hard hat. This is a safety requirement for this job. Let's review the company safety procedures, so you are clear on the rules and my expectations."

2. *A verbal warning with note to the file.* You talk to the employee again. "You are not following company safety procedures, John. This is the fourth time this month you haven't been wearing your hard hat on the job site. You have to wear it starting now, or I'll have to institute discipline up to and including termination."

   Make a dated note that you had this conversation, and drop it in the employee's personnel file. No employee signature is needed at this point.

3. *A written warning.* At this point you are beginning the documentation you will need if you have to terminate the employee. Unfortunately, people are in love with litigation, so this stuff is needed. The written warning goes like this. "This note is a formal warning to John concerning company safety procedures. He has not worn his hard hat on the job site on the following dates and times (Document them). The company safety procedures are in writing, and John has access to them, has read them, and has signed a copy of them. I have reviewed these procedures with him on these dates (Document these, too). In addition, I gave John a verbal warning on (date). Company policy for failure to follow safety procedures includes termination. I need to see immediate compliance with company safety polices or discipline may occur up to and including termination." This note needs to be dated and signed by both the supervisor and the employee. If the employee refuses to sign, have a witness sign the note stating that the employee refused to sign the warning.

The goal is to let the employee know the seriousness of the problem and what you are prepared to do if the problem is not addressed.

4. *Leave without pay.* This can be a very powerful attention getter. Remember, since the employee is already on notice with steps one to three above, the next violation can result in discharge, and that may be the most appropriate next step.

    Given that, the next time you are on the job site and John is without his hard hat, tell him to leave the job for the remainder of the day and the next day or two. Tell him to think about whether or not he wants this job. Require that he meets with you before going back to work. Discuss with him the problem and the consequences once again. Document the leave and the conversation. Legally, if he leaves in the morning, you have to pay him for half the hours he was supposed to work on that day. If he is asked to leave in the afternoon, you owe him for the full day. Send him home anyway. Making an employee leave the job can be a real wake-up call. I have seen it work wonders. Just having to explain to a spouse why they are home early and being home for a few days with nothing to do but think can be a real behavior changer!

5. *Termination.* In front of a witness, notify the employee orally and in writing that he is no longer employed as of (date). Have all wages due the person in hand. Retrieve from him all company keys, tools, and supplies. Do all the legal requirements — these vary by state. Do not let the employee finish the workday. The last thing you want is a workers' comp claim as they walk out the door, or have them complaining to other employees about you and the company. What you want is them gone! It may be necessary in some cases to escort the employee to their vehicle. Keep their personnel file safely locked up. You may need all that documentation in the future.

Then close your door and think about what you could have done differently to have prevented the need for the termination. Maybe you should have checked references better, trained sooner, or discussed the problem earlier. Regretfully, maybe there was nothing you could have done that would have made a difference. If you gave John comprehensive performance reviews, followed up with your expectations, and were clear with consequences, then don't beat yourself up. If you did your part, then in reality, you did not fire him; he *chose* to leave, because he *chose* not to give you the performance you clearly stated was needed to be successful in your company. It is not your fault he no longer has a job, or that he may have a hard time paying his bills. He made his decision on how he wanted to perform, and you made yours. So leave it and move on. Oh, the joys of leadership!

Your "TO DO" List

Staying Legal

1. Do you have personnel policies? Are they accurate, legal and comprehensive? When was the last time they were professionally reviewed? What is their internal marketing potential?

2. Organize your personnel files. When was the last time you reviewed them for completeness?

3. Have you had to discipline or fire an employee? Did you do it right?

4. Are you avoiding dealing with employee problems? The sooner you handle the problem, the better.

5. Are you still fretting over your last disciplinary action? If you can do better next time, do it. If you did your best, don't beat yourself up.

Chapter 12

Now You Have to Sell It

If the creator had a purpose in equipping us
with a neck, he surely meant us to stick it out.

— Arthur Koestler (1905-1983)

Who? Me? I'm Not a Salesperson!!

Remember way back in Chapter One — the list of things on the owner's job description? Well one of the things, #12 to be exact, is "Assuring there is adequate work to meet company needs." Put another way, this means you must ensure the sale of your company's product or service. This most likely means *you* get to be at least one of the salespeople in your company. Yet, many business owners, while great at creating a product or providing a service, hate going out and actually selling it. Why is this?

Well, for starters, what images come to mind when you think of a salesperson? In my workshops I hear such things as — pushy, unethical, slippery, aggressive, white shoes, plaid pants, selling someone something they don't need, phone calls at dinner time, and worse! We carry around in our minds some very negative images of salespeople. But sales, when done ethically, is an honorable profession.

Answer the following questions:

◆ Do you have knowledge, skills, and experiences you can use to guide people towards good decisions?

♦ Are you able to analyze a situation and come up with a solution?

♦ Are you good at persuading people to consider various options before they make a final decision?

If you answered yes to these questions, then you are a good salesperson. A good salesperson identifies a need, assists in finding a solution, and then recommends the best company to fill the need — YOURS! Understand? It is a salesperson's obligation to help people get what they need. By thinking of sales in this way, it gets easier to do. It also gets easier when you realize that sales is a skill that can be learned, and like any skill, the more you practice it, the better you get.

Before we discuss sales any further, please review the idea of *competitive position* on pages 74 to 76 in Chapter 6: "Planning Your Future." Before you can go out and sell, you need to know who you are and why you are different from your competition. You have to know this without thinking about it. When someone asks you what makes your company different from the one down the street, you want to have a precise answer ready. Take some time and review your competitive position. Write down what makes you different and unique. Everyone in your company needs to know this as well, because everyone in your company is a part of the sales process.

Moments of Truth

Jan Carlzon, in his book, *Moments of Truth*, defines "moments of truth" as each individual interaction a customer has with a company. These include the first contact to the last. Contacts like how the telephones are answered, how the actual sale is managed, how payments are handled, how any problems are managed, etc. A happy customer can become an unhappy customer at any given instant. Since reselling to existing customers takes much less time, energy, and money, you want all your customers to have a positive experience at all times. This requires that you and your employees effectively manage every customer interaction. You can be the best salesperson in the world, but the sale, and more important, the resell or referral, can be lost if the customer does not have a positive experience at each level of contact.

Take some time with your staff and identify these points of customer interaction. Then work to improve each one 10%. It's said that it is better to improve 10 things 10% than one thing 100%. It certainly applies here. Periodically have someone "secret shop" your company. Have them call in, stop by, interact with each of your "moments of truth," and then give you feedback. Then improve again and again.

Your customers are also influenced by your sales tools. These include such things as your brochures, letterhead, business cards, advertisements, vehicles, and you and your people's appearance. Look at all your sales tools and be sure they, and your business, reflect who you are in the marketplace. For example, if you are positioning yourself as a high-end builder, or boutique, or bakery, etc., then everything you do, and all the customer sees and experiences, needs to be high-end.

What Makes a Star Salesperson?

A great salesperson may be born, but most great salespeople are made. Five things that make a salesperson great are:

1. *Empathy*. This is the ability to walk in another person's shoes. A great salesperson has a sincere interest in helping the customer. To find the best solution, a good salesperson takes the time to thoroughly understand what the customer needs and what problems must be overcome.

2. *Ego*. A great salesperson has to be able to handle rejection. You will not get every sale you go after. Don't take it personally.

3. *Ethics*. A great salesperson is ethical. They never sell something to a client that the client doesn't need or that doesn't take care of the problem. Enough said.

4. *Market knowledge*. A great salesperson really knows their product, the market, the industry, and future trends. Only then can they truly help the customer.

5. *Training*. Great salespeople never stop learning about their product, about their industry, and about themselves.

Sales Basics

Selling is statistical in nature. You will not get every sale you go after. Because of this, it is important to track the number of sales you make for the amount of effort you expend. This is called your closing ratio — the number of sales versus the number of sales presentations (sales proposals). By tracking this ratio you will see how many presentations you need to make to generate the sales you need for your company to be successful. It also helps you to deal with the rejection inherent in selling. For example, if you have established that you get one sale for every five proposals, then you realize that each NO is getting you closer to a **YES!** Keep in mind that good salespeople expect to get several No's, because they understand that if they have a really high closing ratio, they are probably leaving money on the table!

While it is important to track your closing ratio, don't focus all your attention solely on the close. To have success you will need to focus a lot of your attention on what generates the opportunities to make the sale.

Picture a funnel — wide at the top, narrow at the bottom. The top of the funnel reflects all the things you do to make people aware of your business. This creates the opportunities to sell your product or service. These include your Yellow Page ad, any radio, TV, or newspaper ads, your involvement in your trade association or chamber of commerce, your volunteer work in the community, the signs on your trucks, the job site, and on your building, your participation in a leads group, or whatever. As you feed the top of the funnel, you create the opportunities for finding a potential customer.

The list of potential customers will be fewer people than you meet at the top of the funnel — as the funnel narrows, so do the number of interactions. Let's say that all the activity at the top of the funnel creates 15 opportunities to meet with people who may need your product or service. Of these 15 people, ten are interested in seeing your product. Of these 10, five are interested in having you give them a proposal. Of these 5, one person buys. This gives you a 20% closing ratio (one sale/5 proposals).

The key is to focus on the top of the funnel. If you don't, you will have a tube instead of a funnel. The problem with a tube is that if you don't get that one sale, you don't have anything else coming down the track!

The Selling Process

The first step is to figure out what the customer needs. To do this you have to get people to talk to you. The best way to get people to talk to you is to get them to trust you. To get them to trust you, you must establish a rapport.

Establishing a Rapport

There are a variety of ways to establish a rapport. One of the first is to listen to people and to be truly interested in them. Talk about everyone's favorite person — themselves! Have a sense of humor; provide information; find some common ground. People like and are most comfortable around people who are like themselves.

Bear in mind that if you know how people process information, it is easier to give people a sense that you understand them. Let me explain. Each of us has a preferred sense of how we understand and take in information. Some of us like to process information visually — with our eyes, some auditorily — with our ears, and others tactually or kinesthetically — with touch or movement. If you can match your presentation to the customer's preferred way of processing information, they will feel you understand them. How do you find out which process a person uses most? Here are some clues.

♦ Visual People

Their choice of words will tell you a lot. They will use words like **look, show**, or **see**. For example, they will say, "looks good, I see what you mean, show me again, let's take a look at it." The pace of their words tends to be rapid. When they are thinking, they will look upward. Your proposals and brochures will be read.

♦ Auditory People

These people will choose words like **sounds, tell, talk, rings,** or **discuss**. They will say, "sounds good, sounds like, tell me more, rings a bell, talk my ear off, give me a call, let's discuss it." The pace of their words will be rapid. When they pause to think, they will make sounds. They will grunt or hum. When thinking, their eye movement is to the side, toward the ears. They will pick up your brochure or proposal, and then set it down and ask you to tell them about it.

♦ Kinesthetic People

Their words might be **touch, hang, get, hold, grip,** or **feel.** They will say, "touch base, hang on, get my arms around it, hold up, come to grips with, get a feel for." The pace of their words will be slower, with silent pauses. They will look down when thinking. Your brochure or proposal needs to have weight (lbs.).

Try this. As you ask a customer what their current problems are, watch their eyes. Since their eye movement is a clue to how they process information, you will know which process they prefer; then you can match your words to their preferred way. For example, if you determine they are visual processors, then during the sale you might say, "Let me **show** you what I can do for you." As the sale continues the customer might respond with, "I **see** what you mean," and then at some point you say, "I'm glad you **took a look** at this; I think you **see** now how I can help you." Matching your customer's language pattern helps you establish a rapport, because they feel you really understand them. For some, this may sound simplistic; it's not. Language patterning is a subtle skill that can dramatically increase your success.

Remember too that communication is only partly what you say. Just as important is the tone of voice you use, your body language, and the look on your face. It's said that a listener's subconscious reading of your body language has 7 times more impact on the listener than what you say. Try to keep these things in mind as you work to establish a rapport with your potential buyer. As you establish a rapport, then determining the buyer's needs becomes easier.

Determining Need

In sales, we often say that people not only buy when they want something but when they have a problem and they are in pain. To determine a customer's needs, ask. Then listen carefully. If you are thinking about a response before they finish speaking, you are not listening. By listening intently you can accurately identify what the customer wants or what is making them uncomfortable. Thus, you are better able to provide solutions. Paraphrase back what you have been told, so that you are clear about what is being said. Stay focused until you truly know what the issue or need is.

Building Value and Creating Desire

Now is the time to educate the buyer about your product or service. Explain why they should deal with your company instead of your competition. This is when you need to know your competitive position (how and why you are different from the competition, pg.71), and be able to articulate it without putting the other guy down. Explain why your service is valuable and what solution it provides. Think in terms of features and benefits.

Features are the specifics of the product or service. Benefits are how the product or service will meet the person's needs. Features on a car are the tires, the engine, or the transmission. The benefits are safe, reliable transportation that has enough power to get you out of trouble, and looks so good it makes you look good. The features of a life insurance policy are the price, how much it pays, and when. The benefits are leaving your family with what they need once you are gone and evidence of your love and caring.

Once you have established a rapport, determined the need, and built the value of your product or service, then you are ready to make the sale.

Making the Sale

To make the sale you have to ask for it. Once you ask, you need to be quiet. Give them a chance to respond. Often, the response will be an objection to buying. Don't see this as a "No". See this as a request for more information.

Be prepared for this moment by knowing what the usual objections are for your business. For example, common objections for your business could be: it costs too much; I need to check with someone else; the timing is wrong; or, I need to shop around. Once you know the standard objections, develop a response to each one. Then practice responding to each one OUT LOUD. You may be the most articulate person in the world inside your head with your self-talk, but if you don't practice the words out loud, when the time comes to respond to the objections, you will be tongue tied.

When the buyer objects, do the following: agree, clarify, and then ask them to buy again. For example, if the objection is, "Oh, you are so expensive." Agree, by saying, "You're right. We are not the least expensive company to buy from." Clarify with, "However, our service, quality, follow-up support (whatever), will save you time and money in the long run." Then go back to the request to buy. "So, do you want to go ahead now?" The request to buy will most likely bring up another objection. Once again, agree, clarify, and close.

Here is a way to practice this skill. Get 3 people together. Assign to each either the role of buyer, seller, or observer. Then go through the steps of establishing a rapport, determining need, building value, creating desire, and making the sale. Have the observer critique the efforts. Then change roles until everyone has a chance to play each part.

Within your business make knowing the response to potential customer objections fun. Ask your employees to respond to an objection when they are walking down the hall, or when you get them on the phone. The goal is to get the response to be natural and forthcoming.

It's all in your mind

Once you have learned basic sales skills, you still need the right attitude. One of the attitudes you need is that it's okay to make money. This sounds silly, but I have worked with more than one business owner who has had a hard time charging what they are worth, or who is reluctant to make the sale because of his or her attitude toward money.

Think about how we sometimes think about money and those who have it — filthy rich, money is evil, rich people are crooks, I will never make any money, money doesn't grow on trees, etc. To be prosperous, you have to first accept that it is okay for you to be prosperous. In the same way, to make a sale you must accept that it is okay to sell. By accepting that sales is honorable, you become a better salesperson. In this area, positive self-talk is critical.

So is the use of visualization. Before you sell, visualize the sale going well. See yourself establishing a great rapport, finding and filling the need, meeting the objections, and making the sale. Do this before your appointment. (I will discuss visualization and affirmations in detail in the next chapter.) This is hard to do if you don't allow yourself time. Never rush to an important sales call and run in mentally and physically undone. Remember, it is your obligation to help the customer fill their need; be prepared and do it right!

Sales is not one thing that you do. It is a combination of things working together. It is the quality of your service or product and your reputation. It is how you look and act. It is how you manage each customer interaction. It is your ability to differentiate yourself from your competition. It is how you manage your customer service. And finally, it is how well you learn the skill of selling. To learn any skill it takes practice. So start practicing today.

Your Sales "TO DO" List

1. Make a list of how you are different from your competition and commit it to memory. Make sure everyone in your company knows it as well.

2. Within your business identify each point of customer contact, and set out to improve each one.

3. Look at your business from your customer's perspective, and make sure there is consistency between what you say and how you look.

4. Track your closing ratios. Figure out how many sales opportunities it will take to meet your sales goal.

5. Evaluate what you are doing to "feed the top of the funnel". Determine what is working and what isn't, and focus on what's working.

6. Practice the skills of an effective sale, from establishing a rapport through making the sale. List your standard objections, and memorize your response to each. Practice them out loud and in a work group of three.

7. Listen to tapes on motivation and sales. Read some of the books in the bibliography on customer service. Keep a positive attitude.

Chapter 13

TAKING THE LEAP

The important thing is this — to be able at any moment
to sacrifice what we are for what we could become.

— Charles Du Bos

It is all up to you now. With all you have learned, you should have a better understanding of what it takes to run a successful company. There's only one more thing you need to know.

It's Your Attitude That Makes the Difference !!!

We all know the importance of a positive attitude. I also know that when faced with the difficulties of business ownership, we all need suggestions and ideas on how to achieve and maintain a good attitude. Here are a few.

A 15 year study of 1600 peak performers from a variety of fields and backgrounds conducted by the Berkeley Peak Performance Center found that one of the keys to peak performance is the willingness to take risks. One of the reasons these risktakers are willing to take the leap is because they have the attitude that every experience, negative or positive, teaches them how to be successful.

For instance, if you are familiar with the Motown music of the 60's (I love it), you know Diana Ross and the Supremes. They are an excellent example of risktakers. Their first nine records were flops. They took risk, after risk, after risk, times nine! Then they had hit after hit and became the hottest female vocalists in Motown. They used their flops to learn the music business and to refine their performance. Their attitude towards risk taking led them to success.

To implement some of the things in this book you must be willing to take on the attitude of a risktaker. Take goals for instance. I find that just the act of setting goals can be scary for some people. If you can think of goal setting as a risk taking situation that leads to success, then it becomes less scary. You need to think as Jim Rohn, an international motivational speaker, suggests that the purpose of a goal is not where you get, but whom you become along the way — what it makes of you as you strive to achieve it.

What this really means is that you need to work harder on yourself than on your job. This is where the attitude of a risktaker takes effect, because you must risk leaving your comfort zones to work on your own personal development. It's a risk worth taking, because if you work hard on your job, you will earn a living, but if you work hard on yourself, you will earn a fortune.

Thus, business development and personal development are two sides of the same coin. Accordingly, your business reflects who you are and how you view the world and the people in it. That's why when you are young and have more energy than know-how, you can run your business on sheer drive and determination. Unfortunately, one day that method no longer seems to work. The attitude of, "I'll do it myself, the hell with everyone else," no longer creates the results you want. How you have always done it, and how that is reflected in your business, is no longer working — for you, your employees, your spouse, for anyone. Besides, you are just plain exhausted, and it is not worth the effort anymore. Your goals have changed, and thus the attitudes you bring to your business must also change.

Now, let's take some slightly different looks at how people see the negative as a positive — how they see risk taking as a requirement for success.

For some, failures that result from risk taking can be devastating and put an end to their efforts. For others, it simply means they have eliminated an option. Thomas Edison is famous for this attitude toward failure. In the early 1900's he was trying to develop a new storage battery. After testing a huge number of possible compounds, upwards of 50,000 by some accounts, someone asked whether he was discouraged by so many failures and his lack of results. His response, "Why, I've gotten a lot of results. I know several thousand things that won't work." To find an answer, Edison knew that he had to risk thousands of hours of his time in a trail and error process. He also knew that to have success he must do it.

Tom Peters, a business management guru, speaks of failing forward — what a great concept. This is the idea that risk taking may not lead you to where you thought you were headed; but, because you take advantage of an opportunity along the way, it creates success. For example, as many people know, the glue that makes 3M's Post-It notes possible was a mistake. The inventor was trying to invent a super holding glue. The inventor failed forward.

Successful people have the attitude that failing is necessary to succeed; indeed, it is part of success. You don't become great, and you don't change your life, without taking risks and using failures.

It is not what happens to you, but how you react to events that will define your future. You make choices all day long on how you will respond to the world around you. You can be a victim or a victor. You can react, or you can create. You can laugh, or you can cry. You can create your future, or you can relive your past. You can bemoan the fact that your business is not meeting your needs and is driving you crazy. Or, you can step out of your comfort zone today, do something differently, and approach your business and your life in ways that will be more effective. What you cannot do is stay the same and expect different results. Einstein said that to do so is the definition of insanity. So, while it may be time to get to work on your business, it is definitely time to get to work on yourself.

As Theodore Roosevelt said, "Far better to dare mighty things even though checkered by failure, than to take rank with those poor spirits who neither enjoy much nor suffer much for they live in a gray twilight that knows not victory nor defeat."

An Approach

The biggest challenge now before you is to begin the process of developing specific techniques that you can use to create the attitude necessary for success. That process starts right between your ears, because the place to start changing is with your thoughts.

It's said that:

Your thoughts create your words

Your words create your actions

Your actions create your habits

Your habits create your character

Your character creates your destiny

Amazingly, human beings think about 50,000 thoughts a day. A university study found that for many people 89% of those thoughts are negative. That equals 44,500 negative thoughts a day. For example — "I can't do that. I really screwed up. I'll never understand my financial information. I don't have time to plan. I'll never get it all done."

Why is this so? A Stanford University study suggests an answer. University students conducted a study in which a group of two-year old children were followed around for the day. The students recorded the negative and positive comments made to the two-year olds. By the end of the day, the students recorded 437 negative comments to 32 positive. It is easy to see why we might have negative thought patterns. We have had plenty of input!

In a very direct way, your thoughts create your reality. If you are thinking negative thoughts about yourself, your business, and the people you work with, there is a strong likelihood that you will end up with negative outcomes. For example, if you wake up in the morning thinking that it will be a lousy day, it probably will be, because that is what you are expecting. You will find *something* that makes it a lousy day. If you expect your employees to screw up that is what they will do. You will see everything they do wrong and little they are doing right. As you sow, so shall you reap.

Changing how you perceive the world, and thus changing your business, starts in your mind. Once again, it starts with setting some goals, writing them down, and reviewing them. Part of the review process is internal. You need to form positive visualizations in your mind. You need to envision in your mind's eye what you want — see it, feel it, taste it, and smell it. Whether is it is more free time, more prosperity, or more repeat business, you need to imagine yourself having it.

You also need to make verbal affirmations about your goals, saying them over and over in your mind. To do this effectively, your affirmations need to be positive, personal, and in the present tense. They need to state what you *want* to happen, not what you *don't* want to happen. You need to affirm it happening for you right now, in the present.

Repeat your affirmations throughout the day, particularly when you get up in the morning and before you fall asleep at night. In this way, your conscious mind will be tuned to what you want, and if an opportunity occurs you can instantly grasp it. Your subconscious will also be at work on the problem, creating or realizing solutions. Replace some of those old negative thoughts with positive ones, and you'll be amazed at what transpires.

Do this and you will better understand why (as you might have expected) a longitudinal study done by Yale University proved that attitude was a major key to people's success. Positive affirmations and visualizations will help you to have the positive, "can do" attitude that is the basis of success.

One Last True Confession

Besides making more money and having more fun, I have other reasons for wanting you to **Run Your Business So It Doesn't Run You.** I think that if your business is well run and profitable, then you have more time to take care of yourself, your family, and your community.

We are more than who we are at work. We are parents, spouses, siblings, aunts, uncles, cousins, friends, teammates, intellects, lovers, and more. What is it you love to do? How long has it been since you've done it? Whatever it is, make time for it. Is it getting in shape? Coaching your kid's softball team? Learning a new skill? Seeing the world? Speaking a foreign language? Restoring a car or home? Meditating, praying, or thinking new thoughts? Take time to take care of your needs, and you will find that you are more effective in all areas of your life.

What about your families? Your kids need you. We read too frequently about teenage apathy, or kids without parental guidance headed for trouble. Not my kid? Do you spend enough time with them to know? Organize your business week so you can spend more time with them. They need you in their lives. They need you to tell them when they are doing great and when they need to straighten up and fly right. They need your love and your rules. You need to participate actively in their lives, day in and day out.

And what about your spouse? They need your love and attention too. Make time for your love relationship so that it grows and is long lasting. Take time to say "I Love You" and make every hug count. Success without love is pretty hollow. Spend the time to ensure that you have a successful family as well as a successful business.

And finally, your community needs you. Our businesses are successful because they exist in supportive communities. Show your thanks by giving back to your community. I ran a successful nonprofit corporation for 10 years. One of the reasons it was successful was because of the support it received from the community of Sebastopol, Ca. People gave of themselves in many ways — remodeling facilities, raising money in the annual membership drive, and becoming friends with the people we served. There are many ways to get involved — Chambers of Commerce, city councils, church groups, service clubs, or individual contributions. There are many community needs waiting to be filled with your talents. Reach out and find a cause that fills your heart and satisfies your soul. Everyone, including you, will be better and stronger for your service.

Time for You to Take The Leap

Tom Watson Sr., founder of IBM, said, "If you want to be the greatest company you have to start acting like one today." So figure out what your great company will look like, and see yourself there. To create the synergy to move forward, communicate your vision to the people around you. Give up the easy way, create those magnificent failures; learn and grow, and your business will grow with you. Life is too short. Have fun. Do what you love and enjoy every moment of it.

We have come to the end of this book on how to run your business. I hope you can turn to any of these chapters to get direction on what you need to do *now*. I hope that you are ready to plan your future and the future of your company and will do so by balancing all the aspects of your being. I hope that you see your employees as your company's most valuable asset and will form a partnership with them, so that they too can enjoy the journey and share in the success.

The simplest step *you* can take is the one within your mind, the one that says *you can and will* manage your business differently — *you are* successful and profitable, and *you are* having fun. It is just a matter of taking one step at a time to make it a reality. The path is right here. Start walkin'.

> *A man is a success if he gets up in the morning and gets to*
> *bed at night and in between he does what he wants to do.*
>
> — Bob Dylan

"TO DO" List

Taking the Leap

1. Think and act positively.

2. Write your goals, review them, visualize them, and affirm them.

3. Act like whom you want to be, and decide where you want to be.

4. Fail forward!

5. It's time to do it — start walking, one step at a time.

> *Whatever your mind can conceive and believe, your mind can achieve.*
>
> — Napoleon Hill, *Think and Grow Rich*

GLOSSARY

Aging reports: Two reports, one of which tracks the status of your accounts payable, and the other, your accounts receivable in terms of current, 30, 60 and 90+ days past due. A part of your management information system.

Affirmations: repeating in your mind's eye what you want to happen to you and doing so in the present tense.

AM Huddle: A quick, no coffee, no donut daily meeting with people whose jobs support and interact with each other, with the goal of better support and understanding and fewer interruptions as the day proceeds.

Arbitration Policy: A legal and speedy way of resolving disputes between employees and employers outside the court system, whereby the issue is submitted to an arbitrator instead of a judge and jury.

Assets: What you own; they are reflected on the Balance Sheet in three types: *current assets* are ones that can be easily liquidated, *fixed assets* are ones that are a permanent part of the business, and *other assets* which are ones with nowhere else to go.

At Will Statement: A part of a company's personnel policy which, in legal language, says the employee/employer relationship can be terminated at any time with or without cause.

Attitude: One of the most important ingredients in a successful business or successful life.

Balance Sheet: The financial picture of your business at a given moment of time which lists assets, liabilities, and capital. A part of your management information system.

Benefits: 1) The health plan, vacation, holidays, sick leave, or other benefits you provide for your employees. These help you attract and keep great employees and are part of your *internal marketing* program. 2) A sales term for how a product or service will meet a person's needs.

Budget: The financial plan for the business reflected as total annual sales, expenses, and profits, and showing these numbers spread over twelve months. A part of your management information system.

Capital: What some accountants refer to as the difference between assets and liabilities. You find it on your balance sheet

Cash Flow Projection: A continuing, rolling, weekly projection of when your money will come in and when it will go out, for a period of time up to thirteen weeks depending on the type of business; used to help you make short-term and daily decisions on where to spend your precious cash.

Chain of Command: Who supervises whom as shown on an organization chart.

Closing ratio: the ratio between the number of sales calls or proposals to the number of sales made.

COGS: Acronym for Cost of Goods Sold. These are costs that directly relate to producing the product or service and are only incurred if the sale is made; also called direct or variable expenses.

Communicator: A time management tool used to avoid interrupting yourself and others by writing down what needs to be communicated to specific people and then scheduling a mini-meeting (or organized interruption with that person) when you get three to four things on your list.

Competitive Position: How and where you position your company in terms of pricing, customer base, and your competition.

Depreciation: Tax voodoo that expenses assets over time in a variety of ways. Talk to your accountant.

Delegation: A learned skill — You give people around you additional responsibilities, often accompanied with training, so that you can accomplish the vital things on your "to do" list.

Direct Expenses: These are expenses that directly relate to producing the product or service and are only incurred if the sale is made; also called variable expenses or COGS.

Dreaded 15 Minute Time Analysis: A useful time management tool to analyze how you spend your time by tracking it in fifteen-minute increments.

Equity: What you have invested in the businesses and what the business owes the owner.

Exempt or nonexempt from overtime: Federal Department of Labor regulations on who gets and who does not get paid for overtime. It also varies by state and is based on specific job requirements, not by whether someone is paid by the hour or the month.

Failing Forward: A term coined by Tom Peters on the importance of failing in order to make progress — taking advantage of mistakes and failures by learning from them or letting them open new doors for you.

Feature: a sales term which refers to the specifics about a product or service.

Feeding the sales funnel: all the activities that create the opportunities to sell your product or service.

Fixed Costs: Expenses such as rent and utilities that occur whether any sales occur or not and do not vary month to month; also called overhead and indirect costs.

Games: A concept in open book management of creating a program to impact your business and its profitability in a positive way.

Gross Profits: Sales minus COGS

Gross Profit Margin: Sales divided into gross profits reflected as a percentage; an extremely important number to know and monitor because it reflects your profitability.

Hiring: One of the most important things an owner or manager does.

Hourly: A way to pay people by the hour rather than by the month. It must not be confused with being nonexempt for overtime.

Income: All money into your business via sales or other sources other than loans.

Indirect Costs: Expenses that occur whether any sales occur or not, and which do not vary month to month, such as rent and utilities; also called fixed and overhead costs.

Internal Marketing: Marketing to the people within your company, reminding them of what a great place it is to work and the benefits that you provide.

Interruption Analysis: Looking at your interruptions in the aggregate so you can spot trends, people or processes that need to be addressed, enabling you to reduce the number of interruptions in your day.

Job or Product Costing: A financial report that tells you how your actual costs are stacking up against what you bid or expected the product to cost. A part of your management information system.

Job Description: A clear description of job expectations for an employee; part of the hiring process and the heart of performance reviews.

Leadership: One of the jobs of an owner of the business; having the vision and the plan, securing the resources to carry out the plan, inspiring and motivating others to realize the vision.

Liabilities: What you owe; they are listed on your balance sheet and come in three types: *current* liabilities are ones that you expect to pay back within a year, *long term* liabilities are ones you will pay over a longer period of time, and *loans payable* liabilities are debts to owners, partners, or share holders.

Management: A hat many owners must wear in their business; carrying out the mission and the plan, implementation, effective use of resources, following through.

Management Information System: Financial information vital to your understanding of what is occurring within your business. Consists of your profit and loss statement, balance sheet, budget, variance report, aging reports, and job costing information.

Mission Statement: A succinct statement of who you are, what your company believes in, and how you operate — all in a few sentences.

Moment of Truth: each individual interaction a customer has with your company and the title of a book by Jan Carlzon.

Net Profit: The amount remaining after all expenses ¾ direct and overhead — have been met. The difference between total sales minus all costs.

Objections: A sales term for the way a customer requests more information.

Overhead: Expenses that occur whether any sales occur, such as rent and utilities. These expenses do not vary month to month; also called fixed and indirect costs.

Pavlov: A Scientist who worked on stimulus/response mechanisms with dogs. Fed after a bell was rung, his dogs salivated whenever they heard a bell.

Pay Schedule: The pay range of who is paid what. It is based on what each job contributes to the company's ability to produce the product or service.

Perfect Week: A time management tool that creates a template of your week attuned to your priorities, as opposed to reacting to what occurs as it occurs.

Performance Reviews: Annual evaluation of employees by their supervisor. The supervisor tells the employee what the employee is doing well and where the employee needs to improve; includes a time-framed plan for making improvements and a follow-up schedule. The review is based on the written, company job descriptions.

Personnel Policies: Legal documents describing policies within your company which relate to your employees, employment practices, benefit program, and other issues and expectations.

Progressive Discipline: Dealing with employee problems through a series of escalating steps, from a verbal warning to written warning, time off without pay through termination. The progression may or may not be followed depending on company policies and the nature of the employee problem.

Procrastination: Putting things off for a variety of reasons, such as fear, overwhelming tasks, boredom, laziness, etc. To overcome procrastinating, first determine its source, then apply the appropriate solution.

Profit and Loss Statement: Also called an income statement. This gives you a picture of your business over time, preferably one month and year-to-date with prior year comparisons; a summary of income, expenses, and overhead. A part of your management information system.

Ratios: A way to evaluate how things are going in your business based on information from your financial statements, often in comparison with industry standards.

Salaried: A way to pay people by the month rather than by the hour. Must not be confused with being exempt from overtime.

Salesperson: someone who identifies needs, assists in finding a solution, and recommends the best resource to fill the need.

Scoring: A concept in open book management of tracking critical information and communicating it to your employees in an effort to move your business numbers in a positive direction.

Span of Control: The number of people one can effectively supervise. This varies depending on the type of business and type of work being supervised.

Stake: The concept in open book management of giving everyone in a company an opportunity to financially benefit from working together to make the company more profitable.

Thirty percenters: The percent of employees who are hard working, heads up, go for it, self-motivated individuals. The ones you want to attract.

Time Management: The process of taking control over how you spend your precious time so you can use it to accomplish your goals instead of someone else's.

Urgent: Those things that demand your time and energy but will not move you toward accomplishing your goals.

Variable Expenses: These are expenses that directly relate to producing the product or service and are only incurred if the sale is made; also called direct expenses or COGS.

Variance Report: A column shown as a percentage on your P&L that tells you how you are actually doing in relationship to your budget. A part of your management information system.

Visualizations: seeing what you want to happen so vividly in your mind that you not only see it but hear it, taste it, smell it, and touch it.

Vital: Those things on your "to do" list that when accomplished *will* move you toward accomplishing your goals.

W.O.T.S UP: Acronym for Weakness, Opportunities, Threats and Strengths; a process for doing your annual planning.

Your Brain: Your appointment book, when it is properly used to keep track of everything you do and when it is used as a tool to help you organize your time.

BIBLIOGRAPHY

General Business

The Deming Management Method, May Walton (Perigee Books, 1986). An overview of Deming's TQM philosophy.

The Effective Executive, Peter Drucker (Harper Row, 1966.) Drucker identifies and discusses the five practices essential to business effectiveness. A business classic, as are any of Drucker's works.

The Great Game of Business, Jack Stack, with Bo Burlingham (Doubleday/Currency, 1992). Using his company, Springfield Remanufacturing Corp. as the example, Stack explores and explains open book management, or as it is called at SRC, the great game of business.

Growing a Business, Paul Hawken (Simon and Schuster, 1987). A good general all around book on managing and growing your business.

If it Ain't Broke . . . . Break It and other Unconventional Wisdom for a Changing Business World, Robert Kreigle and Louse Patler (Warner Books, 1991). Discusses the need for unconventional thinking in rapidly changing times.

In Search of Excellence, A Passion for Excellence, Thriving in Chaos, Tom Peters *et al* (Warner Books). Peters' books are also classics, filled with lots of examples on business excellence.

Leadership and the New Science, Margaret J. Wheatley (Berrett-Koehler, 1994). The application of ideas from modern physics to business management and the need to view business as a dynamic organism.

Open Book Management: The Coming Business Revolution, John Case (HarperBusiness, 1995). A good overview of the how's and why's of open book management with lots of examples.

Bibliography

The Republic of Tea, Mel Zeigler, Pat Zeigler and Bill Rosenzweig (Doubleday, 1992). Describes the start up of a tea company via letters, faxes and the development of a partnership. Zeiglers were the founders of Banana Republic.

Sam Walton: Made in America. Sam Walton (Doubleday, 1992). Walton's bibliography filled with philosophy and sound business advice.

Zapp! The Lightning of Empowerment, William C. Byham (Ballantine Books, 1988). The nuts and bolts of TQM told as a fable.

Leadership And Customer Service

Customers for Life, How to Turn that One-Time Buyer into a Lifetime Customer, Carl Sewell (Currency Books, 1991). A very readable book on the excellent customer service practiced at Sewell Cadillac.

How to Win Customers and Keep Them for Life. Michael LeBoeuf (Berkeley Books, 1988). A great hands-on book on customer service. Easy to read and very practical.

Leadership is an Art, Max DePree (Dell Publishing, 1989). The book is about "the art of leadership: liberating people to do what is required of them in the most effective and humane way possible" and about the servant leader.

Moment of Truth, Jan Carlzon (Ballenger Publishing, 1987). Great book on leadership, empowerment and customer service told by the person who turned Scandinavian Airlines around.

Other

Living Your Life Out Loud. Padi Selwyn and Sally Raspberry (Pocket Books, 1995). How to unleash your creativity with lots of examples and exercises.

The Popcorn Report and *Clicking,* Faith Popcorn (Harper Collins, 1991, 1995). Popcorn is a futurist and trend spotter. Good ideas on where to take your business in the future.

ABOUT THE AUTHOR

Linda Leigh Francis, with a Masters Degree in Education, began her business advertures by administering and helping to develop *The Middle Way*, a nonprofit corporation serving developmentally disabled adults in Sebastopol, Ca. Under her direction the business expanded to include a 24-hour residential care facility and a work training program with three business endeavors: a full-service landscape operation, an organic farm and nursery, and a gift shop.

In 1989, Linda began her work as a business consultant. Since then, she has consulted with and has trained hundreds of businesses ranging from family run businesses to national corporations in construction, manufacturing, service, mail order, real estate, nonprofit agencies, and more. She has served as a Corporate Board member for an international renewable energy and mail order company. Linda, a member of the National Speakers Association, also frequently speaks at national conventions and associations.

Throughout her work, Linda incorporates her life philosophy of care and support for individuals and the community. Linda believes that by running your business well, you can take better care of your family and community.

Thus, Ms. Francis' book, *Run Your Business So It Doesn't Run You*, not only supports her workshops and seminars in content, practicality and humor, it also supports her passion and goal of showing people who are great at their skills and profession how to be equally great at running their businesses and how to be more sane and profitable in the process.

For Additional Copies

You can order additional copies of this book by phone, fax, or mail. Please inquire for quantity discounts. For information on seminars, workshops and presentations, call Linda Francis at (707) 485-0162 or e-mail her at: lfrancis@pacific.net **For cassette tapes please call.**

Phone orders: (800) 222-0666 (Please have your VISA or
                             Master Card ready.)

On-line orders: jpack@pacific.net

— —

Fax order:(707) 485-7071

Please send _____ copies of **Run Your Business So It Doesn't Run You** @ $24.50 per copy + shipping (As of this printing, priority mail is $3.20 for one or two books.) Inquire for quantity discounts. California residents, please add $1.78 per book for sales tax.

Card No: _____Expiration Date:_____

Signature:_____

Name:_____

Address:_____

City: _____ State: ___Zip: _____

Phone:_____

Shipping information (if different from above)

Name:_____

Address:_____

City: _____ State: ___ Zip: _____

Please clip or photocopy this form